"During this incre(
longer deny the change:
our own lives, Dr. Constance Clancy-Fisher's book provides us
with an invaluable step by step guide to land successfully on
our feet happily ready for the new challenges."

Dr. Anne Brown, author of
Backbone Power the Science of Saying No

"*The Gift of Change* is a wonderful gift for all of us who
are *truly* ready to stop resisting change, completely reframe our
relationship with stress, and start living the life we were meant
to live. Whether you are experiencing stressful change in your
love life, your health, or your work; *The Gift of Change* is
the perfect next step to crack the code on how to embrace the
challenge of change. Dr. Connie is a gifted therapist, guide, and
friend who has spent a lifetime developing her unique 5-step
approach to empower you to shift your relationship with life
itself to feel more whole, creative, and radically alive."

Paul Taylor, CEO, Founder Global Citizen Consulting,
former Global-VP, The Coca-Cola Company

the *Gift* of
Change

EMBRACING CHALLENGES TODAY
FOR A PROMISING TOMORROW

Constance Clancy-Fisher, EdD

BALBOA.
PRESS

A DIVISION OF HAY HOUSE

Copyright © 2013 Constance Clancy-Fisher, EdD.

All rights reserved. No part of this book may be used or reproduced by any means, graphic, electronic, or mechanical, including photocopying, recording, taping or by any information storage retrieval system without the written permission of the publisher except in the case of brief quotations embodied in critical articles and reviews.

Balboa Press books may be ordered through booksellers or by contacting:

Balboa Press
A Division of Hay House
1663 Liberty Drive
Bloomington, IN 47403
www.balboapress.com
1-(877) 407-4847

Because of the dynamic nature of the Internet, any web addresses or links contained in this book may have changed since publication and may no longer be valid. The views expressed in this work are solely those of the author and do not necessarily reflect the views of the publisher, and the publisher hereby disclaims any responsibility for them.

The author of this book does not dispense medical advice or prescribe the use of any technique as a form of treatment for physical, emotional, or medical problems without the advice of a physician, either directly or indirectly. The intent of the author is only to offer information of a general nature to help you in your quest for emotional and spiritual well-being. In the event you use any of the information in this book for yourself, which is your constitutional right, the author and the publisher assume no responsibility for your actions.

Any people depicted in stock imagery provided by Thinkstock are models, and such images are being used for illustrative purposes only.
Certain stock imagery © Thinkstock.

Printed in the United States of America

ISBN: 978-1-4525-6835-5 (sc)
ISBN: 978-1-4525-6836-2 (e)
ISBN: 978-1-4525-6837-9 (sc)

Library of Congress Control Number: 2013902692

Balboa Press rev. date: 2/13/2013

Table of Contents

Disclaimer

THIS BOOK DOES NOT SUBSTITUTE for professional, therapeutic or medical advice.

The author and the publisher specifically disclaim any liability, loss, or risk, personal or otherwise, that might be incurred, directly or indirectly, through the use and application of any of the content of this book. All matters regarding your emotional health and that of your family require the medical and/or psychological consultation and supervision of a competent psychotherapist and/or medical doctor.

The names and identifying characteristics of the individuals referred to in examples in this book have been changed for confidentiality purposes and protection of their identity.

Acknowledgments

I AM TRULY GRATEFUL TO everyone who helped and supported me with the creation of this book.

First of all, I want to thank my husband, Robert Fisher, D.C., Dr. Bob, for his incredible wisdom, gift of words, and organization. I could not have completed this book without him.

Bob took a lot of his valuable time, when he could have been doing other things much more fun, to read and reread my material and help me shape it so that it would be clearer to the reader. His tireless efforts and invaluable suggestions truly made my vision for this manuscript come alive. Bob, thank you is not enough. You are amazing!

Once in a great while you meet a special teacher, mentor, and accomplished individual whom you feel privileged to know. Brian Luke Seaward, Ph.D. is just that person to me. Luke, many thanks for taking your time to write my foreword. It is a real honor to have you, an amazing gifted author, as a contributor to this book. Your support means everything to me. My sincere thanks.

Special thanks to my dear friend and colleague, Anne Brown, Ph.D., who is the author of a wonderful book, Backbone Power. Anne, your continued help and support has been inspirational. Thank you for sharing your knowledge and writing experience with me.

Much gratitude to Lucas Century, who created the beautiful monarch mandala which made the cover of this book so special.

I am grateful to Laura (Missy) Thorne and Loren Jenkins, whose beautiful home in Old Snowmass, Colorado, is where I spent most of my time writing and completing this project. To sit on the porch and view the beautiful snow-capped mountain peaks, the horses in the pasture, the birds chirping every morning throughout the day, was the most serene experience a writer could only dream of. You made it my reality. Thank you.

I am grateful to my family, friends, and colleagues for their support and encouragement. To all of you: I appreciate your patience when I turned down being with you because I was busy working on this manuscript. You all were very understanding, and I was always full of excitement as we discussed the book in the making. Thank you all.

I want to thank all of my clients, past and present. Your trust and confidence in me has made me so grateful to know you and work with you in the best way for your growth. I have learned so much from you as well.

Last, but not least, thank you, my beloved animals, Anastasia (Ana's Banana's) and Ari (Archie Wiggle Butt) and Snookie, the cat. To have you all by my side as I wrote, waiting ever so patiently for your walk, your meals, and time to play ball, was such comfort. You bring me so much joy and love.

Foreword

By Brian Luke Seaward, Ph.D.

YEARS AGO, I MET THE most remarkable woman. Her name was Nien Cheng. She told me of her personal story, one where, at the age of 56, she was falsely accused of being a spy during Mao Tse Tung's rein of power in Communist China and imprisoned for six and one half years in solitary confinement. Cut off from all of her family and friends and routinely threatened with torture, even death, Nien survived not only to tell her story, but also to become a luminous example of the triumph of the human spirit. One day while sitting in her living room in Washington D. C. she explained to me that there is no word for "stress" in the Chinese language. "We call it opportunity," she said with the hint of a smile on her face. Nien was one woman who knew how to open the door when opportunity knocked. Her release from prison came when President Nixon made his historic trip to China. She was released with several other prisoners as a token gesture of human rights. It didn't take long before she planned her escape to democratic freedom, first in London, then Canada and finally in the United States. She tells her story best in her own words through her best selling book, *Life and Death in Shanghai*. True to the infamous Chinese curse 'may you be born in interesting times,'

Nien reminded me that every age is of great interest. "I never saw this period in my life as a curse, but rather a blessing," she reminded me. There are many lessons I took away from my friendship with this most remarkable human being, not the least of which includes the invaluable human resources of patience, optimism, humor and compassion, all of which she epitomized. I call these traits "muscles of the soul" because I believe that each and every one of us has what it takes to get through any crisis, no matter how big or small. Perhaps more than any other time in the history of humanity, our twenty-first century lifestyles are filled with an abundance of stressful episodes, more commonly known as personal crises. Sages and spiritual luminaries remind us repeatedly that there are two ways you can deal with a personal crisis of stress; either as a victim or a victor. The stories of victims are quite common… and boring. Momentary grieving, over time, becomes a perpetual (and annoying) whine. Caught in a whirlpool of negativity, the victim lives the expression, "once a victim, twice a volunteer."

Conversely, the stories of victors, like Nien, are inspiring, for they not only illuminate the remarkable triumph of the human spirit, but also their fortunes of grace and dignity shed light on our paths as well, making our journey a bit easier. Renowned mythologist Joseph Campbell described these stressful moments as "initiations" on the hero's journey. Each stressor offers a profound learning experience. Moreover, each episode of personal crisis offers us the opportunity to move from a motivation of fear toward a motivation of love. This is the only way for the evolution of the soul growth process to occur. For many this shift appears a chasm too wide to cross; fear often keeps them immobilized. Yet this move, this quantum leap, can be made with the mere turn of a thought; a shift in perception. There are many colors in love's rainbow. The book you hold in your hand is a metaphorical bridge over this abyss. Moreover, this book is a gift; yet reading it is not enough to make the necessary changes to bring your life back to balance. Putting these skills into practice on a daily basis is essential so that you may rise above the fray, and land safely to the other side of the abyss.

Connie is not only a wonderful therapist, but a wise teacher and guide as well. Through these pages she will help you reacquaint yourself with this timeless wisdom that often bears repeating, so that we may each polish the rough edges ofour soul and reveal the beauty that exists in our hearts. The subtle message in this book is to become the victor of your journey.

Like Nien's journey to freedom, your hero's journey is a return home; home being a metaphor for homeostasis or inner peace. Moreover, home is the place where you raise your arms in gratitude and declare a triumphant victory. Coming home is a celebration of the lessons learned in the journey and the sharing of these lessons with others so that we might all benefit.

In the words of so many who await your arrival to inner peace, "welcome home!"

Brian Luke Seaward, Ph.D.
Author of the best selling-book,
Stand Like Mountain, Flow Like Water
Director, The Paramount Wellness Institute, Boulder, Colorado

"The primary cause of unhappiness is never
The situation but your thoughts about it."

ECKHART TOLLE

Introduction

I WROTE MY FIRST BOOK, Surviving Stress with a Healing Heart, in 2000. While making changes for this new book, it occurred to me that certain aspects of Surviving Stress are still pertinent today; however, now more than ever we are in a crisis of change throughout our nation and globally with more uncertainty regarding our future than most of us can remember in our lifetime.

As humans, we tend to be quite resistant to change. We view change as a source of stress. It seems the greater the change, the higher the stress. If we could view change as not a threat but rather an opportunity for growth, then the stress of change would be greatly reduced.

An old Chinese proverb reminds us that change does not have to be a crisis, but a chance for learning and personal growth. Everything changes around us. We cannot hold on to anything. With that in mind, it may be easier to recognize the things that come and go. Our emotions change, behaviors change, actions change, our world changes constantly.

Therefore, stress of change is what's really going on. Many of us have arrived in places we never thought we would be. We got off our path, and we are searching for ways to get back on. Much of America and its people are lost. We have fallen into a dichotomy between where we thought we would be and where we are. What if we could turn back the clock and plan our lives differently? What if when we came to that fork in the road we had taken a different route? A different major, a different career path, a different job, a different spouse, a different road all together? We will never know. What we do know now is that as incredulous as it may seem, all of our decisions, actions, and goals were a part of the plan (our life's plan). We were supposed to take the forks in the road that we did to learn important lessons along our life's journey.

With change more prevalent we are asking ourselves what our future is going to be. Many of us are finding ourselves in disturbing situations we did not expect. We thought our careers, jobs, homes, marriages and retirement were secure. Many of us are finding they are not. We now question if there is a way to finding renewed hope and happiness in life. According to a 2011 Gallup Poll, satisfaction with the economy, government, and morality is much lower than it was in 2008.

As a society we are aware of the many challenges we now encounter. All we have to do is turn on the news and learn about the many issues we face: a failing economy, the housing crisis, the high cost of health care, to the never ending war in Afghanistan with its loss of lives and billions of dollars spent, in some opinions, squandered.

Also ongoing is the medical health insurance issue. Millions of people in the United States have no health insurance and cannot afford it. Countless Americans have had their homes foreclosed upon. So unless you have been visiting another planet, most of us know that our life here on planet earth is one of change, and we are "living in interesting times," the Chinese curse referenced in Dr. Seaward's foreword. Is it any wonder that stress, and its related burnout, is our number one health-related issue? As Americans, we are feeling a real physical, mental, emotional and spiritual breakdown. As a result, there is such little peace and serenity left in our culture. We have literally been invaded by twenty-four/seven technology. Cell phones and computers require substantially more of our time. We are all being exposed to increased violence on TV and in movies, as well as to an incessant barrage of negative news on the news reporting networks. According to a 2007 American Psychological Association Study, three-quarters of Americans experience symptoms related to stress in a given month: 77% experience physical symptoms, and 73% experience psychological symptoms. The study also reports that about half of Americans (48%) report lying awake at night due to stress.

As a psychotherapist/hypnotherapist, I work with clients on "deprogramming the subconscious." What that means is eliminating concepts that no longer serve us.

When these concepts get into the subconscious mind they operate automatically without our awareness. Such as "wildflowers give me allergies" or "I always have to answer the phone or I feel guilty."

Clients generally come to me for guidance with a variety of issues, but stress-related issues and anxiety predominate. We all struggle with repeating old behavior patterns. We all are searching for ways not only to reconnect with ourselves but also to gain a better understanding of significant turning points in our lives that can help us transform stress and fear into courage and confidence. We all could use some direction in bringing more awareness to our consciousness to help decrease suffering and negativity on the one hand and on the other increase joy and optimism in our daily lives.

When I assist the client to achieve a relaxed state designed to foster a healthy and enduring sense of self, I incorporate imagery and hypnotic techniques so the subconscious mind receives, absorbs, accepts and retains pertinent information being suggested for positive change. These techniques assist in releasing self-doubt, cultivate feelings of personal mastery, and encourage present moment awareness and self-acceptance. This creates change on all levels-mind, body, spirit and emotions.

Change begins with opening up your heart and trusting yourself to get beyond fear and uncertainty, allowing you to live fully and receive unlimited inspiration along your life's path. In this book, we will address how to manage the stresses, large and small, that change now and in the future will call for.

So as I begin my writing journey, it is my wish for you to learn to embrace your stress and nourish your heart and spirit to rediscover the joy that has always been there to claim. In this book, I will guide you to the deeper level of awareness that is available to all. As a human being, I have experienced so much in the last decade. I will share important lessons that may be of help to you.

I hope it will be your choice to embrace the many changes all of us will face in this lifetime to manage the stress that accompanies it. Perhaps a starting point would be to accept the premise that our soul is on a sacred journey and change is the soul's way of moving us along our path toward enlightenment. Knowing that, we realize that change is for our greater good. We become inspired and our zest for life reaches a new and more evolved level.

"In order to change an existing paradigm, you do not have to struggle to try and change the problematic model. You create a new model and make the old one obselete. That in essence, is the higher service to which we are all being called."

BUCKMINSTER FULLER

CHAPTER ONE

A Survey of Stress and Challenges For Change

LIFE IS LIKE A HURRICANE. My literal hurricane blew through with Hurricane Charlie on Friday, August 13, 2004.

While spending the summer in Vail, Colorado, enjoying the fresh mountain air and the many summer activities that Colorado has to offer, I was still commuting to my home in Sanibel Island, Florida, to see clients for follow-up appointments on a monthly basis. When I flew to Fort Myers the second week of August 2004, little did I know that I would be spending the week preparing for a hurricane. Most of my clients had cancelled, for they had to make preparations themselves.

Hurricane Charlie, Sanibel Island, Florida, August 13, 2004

I have evacuated about four times in situations when the island was threatened with hurricanes in the previous years, and we were blessed to have escaped any major damage. So as luck would have it, when Charlie was threatening the west coast of Florida, I decided this time to "ride it out" and stay home since the predictions were not for a direct hit. Unfortunately, an hour and a half before the hurricane's arrival, the storm took a turn for the Sanibel-Captiva Islands.

The electricity had been turned off, and my only source of communication was my cell phone. Friends began calling and asking me if there was any way that I could get off the island. They had learned on the weather report that the storm was heading right toward the island and it was a category 4, a major hurricane. I explained why I thought I needed to stay put as opposed to trying to leave. My car might not make it off the island, and I would be stuck here anyway. Also, I didn't think the storm would be that bad. Others were not evacuating, and I just wanted to be in my own home despite the evacuation warnings. The storm did come, and it was so intense that I shut my bedroom door and went into my walk-in closet where there were no windows. The wind howled so intensely that I thought every window would blow out and the roof would come off.

The first twenty minutes seemed like hours as I stood huddled in my little closet and waited nervously until the storm passed. My cell phone worked on and off, and I received calls from friends in other states asking how I was faring.

I asked them, "Do you know when this will be over? It seems like it is taking forever!" I was reassured that it would end soon as they nervously watched the Weather Channel and saw the eye right where I was! It wasn't until later that they all told me how scared they were for my safety and well-being. That was their kind way of saying, "Connie, how could you be so stupid and not evacuate?" I felt like Dorothy in the Wizard of Oz when she landed after the tornado in Kansas. I felt as if I wasn't on Sanibel anymore. I looked out my window and I was disoriented. All the trees were down. I could not open my front door. I saw houses I had never seen from my dismantled porch as I looked down the canal in the back of the house. What had just happened was unbelievable. To

Constance Clancy-Fisher, EdD

get down the stairs I had to clear tree branches, sticks, shingles from my roof. I crawled over fallen trees and debris and made it down the street to the Island Store on the main road across from the beach. A few people walked in and out as I did in a complete daze. No one could really talk since we were all in a state of shock. The owner of the store opened and had ice and supplies for folks who remained on the island. I asked the owner if I could take a disposable camera and pay him the next day. With no electricity and therefore no air conditioning, it did not take long to get hot as blazes. I had candles, a flashlight, and knew which neighbors had stayed to ride out the storm.

We all had a gathering later that evening once the shock had worn off. The next morning I woke up early and decided to explore Captiva since some friends had homes there and would surely wonder how their homes had fared. I could take photos and call them with a report. By the time I crawled over the tree branches and maneuvered by bicycle to get to the beach, the sun was out bright and it was really hot. The beach was free of debris, so off I went biking from Blind Pass where I lived to Captiva Island. By the time I reached Captiva, my face was starting to burn. I had remembered to bring water and the camera but had forgotten sunscreen. I never thought I could be lost on the tiny island, but it was even more devastated and unrecognizable than Sanibel. Trees and cable lines were down everywhere, and I could not determine where I was.

It all looked like a jungle. I finally found one of my friend's homes. A tree had gone through the roof, through the pool screen, and into the pool. It wasn't long before word got around that I remained on the island, and the calls began filtering in that evening. I was getting calls from people I didn't even know who asked if I could check on their homes. Later that evening the National Guard was out. I was stopped on the side of the road by the Sanibel Police and told that the Guard would "hold a gun to my head" (there was a curfew) if I didn't go home. Now if that didn't send off a stress alarm I don't know what could!

I told the officer that I was using my cell phone to return calls and trying to help people who were inquiring about the status of their homes. There was no compassion from the officer. It would take years to repair damaged homes and for the island to begin to look like its old self.

No matter what happens, it is really our attitude toward the event that determines our feelings and how we choose to cope. Many times life can be like a hurricane with its intensity and turmoil. Since that memorable day in 2004, there have been horrific storms, floods, and earthquakes globally where people have lost lives, loved ones, homes and villages; life, for them, seemed as if it would never return to normal. There have been wars and terror attacks with many lives lost. Yet, if one survives such a catastrophe, one's life is changed forever.

I was beyond fortunate. I did not lose my home. Because the devastation overwhelmed the insurance companies, it took over a year for repairs to be made. Luckily, the house was livable, and clearing around the house began within weeks. In the face of adversity, resilience can prevail.

We can choose to view events and changes in life in a positive or negative light. If we choose the positive and accept them as a part of life's journey, then we can move on. Often acceptance may come with residual resistance and therefore can be a work in progress.

Best-selling author and psychiatrist M. Scott Peck discloses in his book, The Road Less Traveled, that "life is difficult." It is inevitable that as we go through life we will face some pain and suffering. There will always be issues we had not anticipated: loss, trauma, financial insecurity, pain, setbacks, grief, and sadness. How we choose to handle these situations may determine how much suffering we endure.

Now more than ever, we live in a society of continual uncertainty and fast-paced changes. We had better have our seat belts securely fastened as we go on this journey. Despite our advances in technology and convenience, we lead even busier and more demanding lives. Jane, for example, is a forty-three year-old housewife and business owner. She and her husband are raising three teenagers. They are all in private school and are involved in several after-school activities. Jane commutes over fifty miles everyday to make sure they get to school and participate in all of their activities. She also owns and manages a retail store and is opening a small cafe within the store. She tells me how busy she is and how it is all she can do to keep up and pay the mortgage. She confesses that she is stressed and exhausted. Her husband is self-employed and has been very successful until the recent economic downturn. She confides how they are struggling to continue the lifestyle they were so accustomed to for years.

While technology is a part of all our lives, one may ask if it has made our lives easier. The Internet is wonderful in many ways, and harmful in others. Internet addiction is as rampant as other familiar addictions. It has become easy for people to get hooked and lose sight of what is really important, like spending quality time with those around you. To understand the source of our stress, we must realize that we are mind, body, and soul. Mind and body were meant to function in harmony with the soul. Over time, mind, body, and soul were separated through conditioning, especially in the West.

The mind was programmed to listen to the advice of teachers, parents, friends government officials, and others, not to the soul. We now can witness what this has done to our world. This disconnect results in a feeling of dis-harmony. As a psychotherapist, clients tell me that while they know they have been blessed with a lot of good in their lives, they feel an emptiness, a void. Our souls have been yearning to reconnect with our minds and bodies and they are now beginning to reunite. Through a multifaceted approach, using techniques such as meditation, deprogramming the subconscious through hypnosis, and counseling, we can address mind, body, and soul to achieve integration. As we integrate, we return to the path of our soul.

Little Stress, Little Change; Big Stress, Big Change

Stress comes in all sizes. There is the small stuff, which most of us would attribute to the daily grind, annoyances like losing the car keys. The coffee maker doesn't work properly and the coffee leaks all over the counter. Beefy, the big bull dog, chases the lady walking her two toy poodles. The laundry piles up. Traffic jams make us late for an appointment. Getting stopped for a traffic violation leaves us frazzled. Having an argument with our spouse leads to increased anxiety. And the best thing that happened was losing four quarters in the soda machine and not getting the soda! Get the picture?

Then there are the much bigger stressors that can wreak havoc on our lives and force us into changes perhaps we didn't even see coming: the threat of losing a home due to foreclosure, which is happening tenfold in our country now; a major health issue that will require much medical attention and no health insurance; inability to pay bills; a lay off with no job in sight; divorce; death of a loved one. These kinds of stressors can limit our ability to make rational decisions and lead to acute as well as chronic health problems.

Anxiety is so prevalent now in our culture that it manifests itself in many psychological and physical changes. We function on overdrive, and our bodies become overstimulated into a hyper state.

Our blood pressure rises, and our heart rate increases. We become adrenaline junkies, needing more adrenaline to keep up the pace. To keep that adrenaline pumping, we can turn on the television with all the cop shows and violence to keep us overstimulated. It has become quite distressing to observe how many people seem to be obsessed with watching violence, suffering and scandals, whether real (there are many) or nightly reality TV, as well as violent movies. According to the Media Awareness Network, media has become more violent, graphic, sexual, and sadistic.

"The Earth Mother and All of Her Creatures Need A Lot of Hope These Days."

DAN FOGELBERG

OUR NATION IS IN FLUX

With our concern over the way the direction of our country is going, we may feel depressed or anxious. Frank Newport, Gallup's editor-in-chief, in a 2011 interview reported that only 16 percent of Americans say they are satisfied with the way things are going for the country.

Facing the worst economic outlook in decades, job seekers are struggling and frustrated, yet trying to be optimistic. Data from the U.S. Census Bureau show that more Americans than ever before, 4.62 million, were living in poverty in 2010. About 6.7 percent of Americans live in deep poverty, below 50 percent of the poverty line, the highest rate ever recorded.

For the most part, we do not think that our children will be better off than we are, nor will the future be better than the past. Many adults are going back to school to further their education, but there is no guarantee of finding employment. According to the Office for National Statistics retirement is becoming passe. Older Americans realize they do not have enough saved and must continue to work. The number of people working past state pension age has nearly doubled in the past 18 years. Approximately 1.4 million above the state pension age were still employed in 2011, compared with 753,000 in 1993.

New research from Georgetown University's Center on Education and the Workforce shows that the unemployment rate for recent four-year college graduates is 6.8 percent--more than 50 percent higher than the overall rate of 4.5 percent for four-year college graduates in general. For those with only a high school diploma the unemployment rate is even higher at 24 percent. College graduates, even students with Ph.Ds, are struggling to find work, and many are even working at bachelor-level teaching jobs. Gallup studies also reveal that negative daily experiences for the employed and unemployed differ with age, with the 18-to-29 year old age group appearing to be the hardest hit.

The Associated Press reported in the spring of 2012 that more than half of America's recent college graduates are either unemployed or working in a job that doesn't require a bachelor's degree. Researchers from Northeastern University, Drexel University, and the Economic Policy Institute, based on data from the Census Bureau's current population survey and the U.S. Department of Labor, found of those who graduated with bachelor's degrees in 2012 under the age of 25, 53.6 percent were jobless or underemployed. There is a sense that regardless of one's education is a great challenge. Many of us are overwhelmed with a sense of powerlessness. The housing market was supposed to improve and it keeps getting worse. The employment rate was supposed to fall and it continues to rise. The Wall Street demonstrations are just the beginning of what may come in our nation. It may be that karma (cause and effect) has come full circle to help us grow. After all, we were the only nation to drop an atomic bomb on another country when there may not have been the need to do so. Sixty years later, scholars still argue about the decision to use the atomic bomb on Japan. According to an article in the New York Times, at one point after the war General Dwight D. Eisenhower bluntly stated, "It wasn't necessary to hit them with that awful thing." The Japanese were already defeated and ready to surrender. The countless wars, the greed, the narcissism in our country has peaked to a level that we may now be feeling their effects.

We are hearing of more childhood and adolescent suicides due to bullying, now called "social combat." Internet bullying has contributed to increased stress and low self-esteem especially with adolescents, and it has even played a role in multiple adolescent suicides. There was a recent suicide of a middle school boy as a result of his being bullied by classmates for being gay. So it is not just the adult population that is feeling stressed. Our children and grandchildren face levels of stress far higher than children did a generation earlier. When I was in middle and high school, my biggest worry was whether I would make the cheerleading squad.

We have major concerns over social and financial conditions globally. While we may be instinctively optimistic, positive and idealistic, those ideal dreams and sense of empowerment are fading fast and we are feeling more of a loss of, rather than a sense of, safety and security. All the more, we feel the increased stress that this produces individually and collectively.

New York Times best-selling author, Carolyn Myss tells how every individual possesses a "sacred contract," an obligation to fulfill a divine destiny, and the vision of our mystic founders. Myss describes how every nation holds an agreement made for the planet's highest good. Each citizen's sacred contract is interwoven with that of his nation. From its inception, Myss explains, the United States has been a great spiritual experiment, an unprecedented evolutionary step forward for human civilization that is both magnificent in its promise and perilous in its dangers. To rescue America from its shadow and rescue its highest potential, Myss explains we must envision how we want this nation to be. We cannot return to the 1950's and 60's era, rather we must realistically envision where America needs to go. There is a calling for people to rethink what's going on in a culture deeply affected by war. We sense deep in our soul that our nation is hurting. The nation that gave birth to freedom needs liberating. Myss suggests we hold the earth in our hands daily and remind ourselves that the power is in our own hands. We can remind ourselves of the power of our own soul. Our soul is always talking to us; it is just that we don't always listen. In meditation we can listen. We have always been courageous and optimistic peoples. We have the ability to help our country achieve its optimum potential. We are the change agents. We must shift self-indulgence, greed and narcissism to self-discovery, simplicity and serving our fellow man.

THE PARADOX OF OUR AGING PROCESS

We have bigger houses but smaller families. More conveniences, but less time. We have more degrees, but less sense; more knowledge, but less judgement. More experts, but more problems; more medicines, but less healthiness; We've been all the way to the moon and back but have trouble crossing the street to meet the new neighbour.

We built more computer to hold more information to produced more copies than ever, but have less communication; we have become long on quantity, but short on quality.

These are times of fast foods but slow digestion; Tall man but short character; Steep profits but shallow relationships. It's a time when there is much in the window, but nothing in the room.

HIS HOLINESS THE 14TH DALAI LAMA

Now over a decade into the twenty-first century, we are faced with a major transformation on all levels: physical, mental, emotional and spiritual. Can we transform our planet and recreate what technology has taken from us? While technology is wonderful in many ways, we have truly lost our humanness. It's quite disturbing to walk into a restaurant and observe four teens sitting in a booth, not speaking to one another for at least 15 minutes because all they are doing is texting. What is the lesson? What is the solution?

The issues above are just a few of the many issues affecting Americans and the world population today. We are being pushed and sometimes forced to return to the basics, the simple truth we need to live by. The rich 80's and 90's are gone. The greed and materialism that contributed to America's meltdown has affected us all in some way and physically wounded many. How do we ever bring our wounded psyches back into balance? How do we learn to manage all the stress in our lives?

Whatever the stressors, large or small, acute or chronic, they all accumulate unless you know appropriate ways to manage. The following questions may provide some awareness of where you are with your current levels of stress and change:

- Are my reactions to stress putting me or anyone else in risk of physical danger?
- Is there anything I can do to keep a potential stressful event from occurring?
- Is this stressful situation out of my control?
- Will there be long-term effects of this stressful situation on my life or the life of others?
- Will becoming upset and angry help the stressful situation?

So what exactly is stress? There are many definitions of stress, and for many of us, stress may be different depending on what is happening in our lives on any given day.

One definition for what we feel when we experience stress is:

"Stress is our ego's response to any real or imagined threat or demand placed upon it."

"Resistance feels like trying to move Forward with the breaks on."

HALE DWOSKIN

ENTHUSIASTIC STRESS

Not all stress is bad! Enthusiasm takes stress to a positive level. If we didn't experience some enthusiasm (positive stress with a goal), we would wake up everyday, put the covers over our head and return to sleep!

The happiest people minimize stressful situations. There is plenty that you can do to minimize stress and its negative effects. Yet most are puzzled about how this can be done. A generally held belief is that our stressful events are generated by events outside of us. If only our spouse, boss, colleagues, parents would change, then we wouldn't have so much stress! Do you find you are still waiting for others to change so you will be happy and less stressed? Much of our stress comes from reacting to outside events rather than going to that inner part of the self and asking how we became so stressed to begin with. The following case illustrates an example of reaction to stress in coupleship:

Client: Bill came home the other night drunk again. I was so enraged with anger I threw a glass at him. It missed him, but I had to do something. I began screaming at him to get out or I was leaving.

He told me to shut up and just played his music as loud as he could to drown me out I guess. I went into the bedroom and locked the door. I put ear plugs in and finally fell asleep.

The next morning, Bill was passed out on the couch. I woke him because I was still so angry. He passively looked at me and then left.

Counselor: Did he return?

Client: Oh yes, later in the day. He was silent, but the pattern of drinking just repeated itself. He is good for a few days; then he starts sneaking the liquor thinking I won't know, but it's so easy to tell he is drinking through watching his behavior. I am really getting sick of this. It is like when I was a kid and my father came home drunk. I watched how my mother dealt with it and now I am doing the same thing.

Counselor: Have you tried talking to him when you both are calmer and he hasn't been drinking?

Client: Yes, and we seem to get along when he is not drinking.

He responds to me lovingly when I talk to him, and I respond lovingly to him just to try to keep the peace.

When he starts drinking, I can't seem to help but react in rage.

Counselor: Have you ever left?

Client: Yes, for the night. I would go get a hotel room and at least get some sleep and peace, but I cannot afford to keep doing that.

Counselor: Why do you stay?

Client: It seems to get better, and I think he will change and we can work it out.

This next exchange is the couple in acceptance mode:

Client: I told Bill yesterday when he was not drinking that I have decided to end the relationship. I was calm and very sad, but after much thought, I decided it was the healthy thing to do if I am ever going to stop enabling and get into a good relationship that I feel I deserve.

Counselor: And how did it go?

Client: He was very shocked that I actually did it, but he responded in a calm way. He said he was going to get help for his drinking and I told him I was so glad for him, but for now, I need to be on my own. It was a peaceful conversation. I also decided that I need to go to Al-Anon per your suggestion. I have to do something so this doesn't happen again. I am so sick and tired of living like this, but I know this is going to be a change for the better. It had to come to this.

While the client has been in other alcoholic relationships, she tells me this is the first one that she could learn to accept rather than react to the situation. She realized that she was the one who had to make the change for growth to occur for her. Her stress had gotten the best of her, and she repeated the behavior of reacting just as she had observed her mother do all those years. The vicious cycle continued as they kept dancing the dance. Finally, the client learned some coping strategies, one of which was to respond to Bill rather than to react, accepting that he was not going to change.

She went to that deeper part of herself, her wise self, and began to explore how she ended up in that situation to begin with. After counseling and much deep inner work, she was able to regain control of her emotional self, end her suffering, and let the relationship go with peace. She regained her enthusiasm for life again.

Stress taken to a higher level becomes enthusiasm. The good news about having enthusiasm is that it leads people to achieve optimum levels of wellness and performance. For example, if you have to give a talk, even a little bit of enthusiasm will help motivate you to be better prepared and help you to speak more clearly.

Some people report that they work best under pressure. If they have a deadline, being enthusiastic about what they are attempting to achieve can be a positive motivator since some people are more apt to get going and complete the task at hand.

It doesn't mean that the actual deadline can't be stressful; it is what you say to yourself about the deadline that will determine your reaction. If my reaction is that the deadline is stressful, this can lead to loss of enthusiasm and an unwanted result. This is when you want to pay attention and become aware of when enthusiasm is turning back to stress.This is a red flag, waving right in front of your eyes indicating trouble ahead. You need to alter this as much as you can before distressing events take the joy out of life.

If you happen to be one of those who feels exhausted, burned out, tired, overwhelmed and ill from all the demands and uncertainty in our world, you are not alone. We tend to believe, as mentioned earlier, comes to us from outside ourselves, such as layoffs, corporate downsizing, outsourcing, financial stress, caring for aging parents, aging, negative news from the media and so on. In truth, stress comes from how we perceive, interpret, judge and behave in situations life presents. Life can be good, bad, pleasurable or painful depending upon your inner thought processes.

"It is difficult to make a man miserable while he
Feels worthy of himself and claims kindred to
The great God who made him."

ABRAHAM LINCOLN

Our self-worth affects how we manage stress. We all have different levels of self worth. The development of our real self-worth comes from the completeness and wholeness within ourselves.

The amount of self-worth that you assign yourself is of great importance. It is important to learn to appreciate yourself every day. The key is to learn to love and honor yourself. Learn to listen to and trust your inner guidance system, that inner knowing that softly guides you to the proper action for the situation you are facing. Your inner guidance (intuition) system will not lead you astray. We all have an inner knowing. It can come as a hunch to take a certain course of action. You may feel a strong sensation in your body to avoid a situation. Pay attention to the messages you are receiving.

I often hear from women that they blame themselves for turning their head and ignoring what their "gut feelings" were telling them. This is common especially in relationship issues. At the beginning of a relationship we are all on our best behavior. There may be little red flags the first few months of the relationship; however, those red flags are quickly ignored because there are too many good things going on. After the fact, when things don't work out, we think, I should have paid more attention to his or her self-absorption, drinking too much, gambling, overspending, stinginess when it comes to the others' needs, not following through on things that were planned, etc. We blame ourselves. Why? Low self-worth. This is how we were programmed. Most likely, this goes back to our family of origin.

Since our early years, we have heard our families tell us how, and what, to think about ourselves. Consider listening to yourself. Stop using low self-worth as an excuse not to live life to its fullest with the utmost self-confidence. Learn to accept situations as they are and consider what is the best appropriate action. Perhaps talking with clergy, a professional counselor or trusted friend can be a start.

So why not choose to trust yourself? People who have a genuine sense of self worth are able to relax and live in the present. They handle stressors with ease. Pay attention to the people in your life who seem to be comfortable with who they are. They have high self-worth and are not overwhelmed with stress and tension. They live in the present moment and do what is necessary for that moment. Now think about those who are stressed out. How would you rate their self-worth? This is not to say that one has to be stress free to have a good self-image. Again, we know that some stress can

Constance Clancy-Fisher, EdD

be helpful because it motivates us to take risks and achieve our goals.

Feelings of self-worth can come and go depending on how well we accept what is going on in our lives.This is a part of being human. Having a sense of purpose in life and living life with a sense of purpose bolsters self-worth. When you allow your self-worth to be compromised, you are not living constructively and stress occurs. Take each moment to feel worthy of your self and your life.

Self-esteem comes from being able to Define the world in your own terms and Refusing to abide by the judgments of Others.

OPRAH WINFREY

How we respond to our stressors can be very revealing as to how well we cope with them. When I was preparing for the hurricane's arrival my fight or flight response kicked in. This response is probably reminiscent of our ancestors who must have reacted this way when faced with the saber-toothed tiger. Back in the caveman days, the hunter would have fought or fled. Physiologist Walter Cannon was the first to describe the "fight or flight" stress response around the turn of the 20th century. He explained it as a series of biochemical changes that prepare you to handle threats or danger.

Our cave dweller ancestors needed quick bursts of energy to fight or flee predators. Obviously, today there are no literal saber-toothed tigers, but there are other creatures that lurk about.

Today's equivalent stresses include unemployment, debt, IRS, unstable weather systems, challenging relationships, work, family, health issues, techno-stress, and fear of the future.

What we often experience are physical symptoms such as muscle tension, headaches, backaches and fatigue.

Emotionally, we may feel sad, uncomfortable, fearful, anxious, worried, and even upset with ourselves for allowing conditions to get to a crisis point. Such symptoms exacerbate current conditions that can lead to further issues later on. For example, research suggests that asthmatics have more asthma attacks when they are stressed.

We are now aware of how stress creates wear and tear on the body. Paradoxically, in this anti-aging culture we inhabit, the more stress, the more we age. We tend to be quite hard on ourselves because of our exceedingly high expectations and the stress they engender. Now more than ever we are working more (unless you are unemployed) to earn enough to pay our mortgages, food, and college expenses for the kids, let alone any enjoyment and entertainment for ourselves.

Physiological Aspects of Stress

The first major researcher on stress, Hans Selye, was able to trace what happens in the human body when stress is encountered, whether from real or imagined threats of danger. The cerebral cortex (the thinking part of the brain) sends an alarm to the hypothalamus (the main switch for the stress response in the midbrain). The hypothalamus then stimulates the sympathetic nervous system to make a series of changes in your body. Your heart rate, breathing rate, muscle tension, metabolism, and blood pressure all increase. Your hands and feet get cold as blood is directed away from your extremities and your digestive system into larger muscles that can assist in fighting or fleeing. You will experience a locking up in the diaphragm as well as butterflies in the stomach. Your pupils dilate, and your hearing becomes more acute. Your adrenal glands begin secreting corticoids (adrenaline, epinephrine, and norepinephrine), which inhibit digestion, reproductive growth, tissue repair, and the responses of your immune and inflammatory systems. These responses can have long-term negative effects if not dealt with because these important functions keep your body healthy.

THE HIGH COST OF FEAR

The only thing we have to fear is fear itself.

FRANKLIN DELANO ROOSEVELT

FEAR CAN LEAD TO FIGHT OR FLIGHT RESPONSE

THE INTRUDER

The following story is the 80's version of fleeing the saber-toothed tiger. Years ago my former college roommate was living in a city in an apartment complex on the second floor. Suzie came home from work on a Friday evening and settled in with her cat. She took a bag of garbage and set it outside her door. She glanced down the stairs only to notice a man looking up at her. She went back inside, locked her door and had an eery feeling. Suzie knew her sliding door lock was broken. She had a hunch to go into her guest room. She noticed her cat sitting below the curtain. The cat moved just enough to displace the curtain, so Suzie looked out and saw a shadow of a person climbing reflected on the next building. This person was climbing to her balcony! Oh, no! she thought. She remained quiet for the moment not really having time to plan what she was going to do next. Her heart was racing as her adrenaline kicked into high gear. She remembered she had a piece of driftwood sitting in a corner by the sliding door.

She tiptoed back into the living room, grabbed the driftwood, slowly opened the slider, and there they were, two hands on the concrete of her balcony. Have you ever wondered if you were in physical danger if you could really let out a scream? Well, Suzie found out. She hovered over the railing, took the driftwood and whacked the guy and let out a blood curdling scream!

The intruder dropped to the ground and took off. Neighbors ran out of their apartments and asked her if she was okay. Unfortunately, the guy got away. Security arrived, but it was too late. Suzie was shaken, but she learned that when faced with danger, her stress fight or flight alarm sounded. She could not flee; therefore, she had to meet her attacker and face her fear for physical survival. Fear is only meant to last long enough to get a person out of danger, and that is all. If we allow this fear to last longer than it should, it can take over and control us. Therefore, we need to know what fear is to allow our emotions and actions to serve us in a healthy way. We need to be aware that fear can also stimulate a self-defeating pattern.

When you experience fear of failure, abandonment, financial loss, health issues, or rejection, your muscles tighten up and your breathing becomes rapid and shallow. Oxygen flow to the brain is lessened and you no longer think clearly. These physical reactions can also result from thinking about our fears, which helps make the worst manifestation of what we fear more likely to become a reality. Remember, what we focus on expands.

THE RELAXATION RESPONSE

Dr. Herbert Benson, who coined the term "relaxation response,"

Constance Clancy-Fisher, EdD

suggested that you can use your mind to change your physiology for improved health and even reduce your need for medications. To begin the relaxation response, focus on your breath. Practice breathing diaphragmatically (belly breathing). Imagine inhaling relaxation through the stomach, diaphragm and lungs; then imagine exhaling stress and tension you have carried in your mind and body. The breath is a life force that keeps you centered in the present moment. This is why the relaxation response is so important. The same mechanism that turned your body's stress response on can turn it off. When you decide that the real or imagined situation is no longer a threat, your brain stops sending emergency signals to your brain stem, which in turn ceases to send panic messages to your nervous system. Several minutes after you shut off the danger signals, the fight or flight response burns out. Your metabolism, breathing rate, heart rate, muscle tension and blood pressure all return to the levels they were before the incident. So the relaxation response is to this day very useful as a natural restorative process.

ACUTE STRESS

While my husband and I were spending our summer vacation in Old Snowmass, Colorado, we often spent our days hiking on beautiful scenic mountain trails. One day, our two yellow labs, Ana and Ari, set out with us for a beautiful hike on a quiet remote trail. We were about an hour into our hike and close to a beautiful waterfall, when suddenly our dogs took off and began barking. Bob was ahead of me and was quick to shout, "There's a bear!" I quickly got the bear bell out of my pack and started shaking it and telling the dogs to "get back here!" I just heard the shuffle in the woods and saw a quick shadow of something running off. Bob had gotten a much closer look at the bear and said that he had gotten up on his hind legs. The dogs subsequently stopped in their tracks and ran the other way back toward me. Fortunately for us, the bear ran off in the other direction. That was a fight or flight moment. While we know there are bear in the woods, seeing one so close was not to be forgotten. So if we are nature lovers and outdoor enthusiasts, we may experience the cave dweller stress along with the civilized modern day stress such as traffic jams and road rage! What I described in the above event was acute stress. It comes on quickly and disappears usually within twenty minutes.

Acute stress can be intense but short-term. Another example of acute stress occurs when you are pulled over for a traffic violation. You hear a siren and look in your rear view mirror. You see the flashing lights of a police car, your heart rate goes up, your blood pressure rises, and you panic about the possibility of getting a ticket. Once you have experienced the initial hassle, you return to homeostasis and all is okay.

CHRONIC STRESS

The other side of the coin is chronic stress. This can be something more long-term such as on-going difficult relationship issues, unemployment, life-threatening illness and many other unrelenting stressors that last much longer than acute stress. Chronic stress can wreak havoc on our bodies. It can accelerate the aging process by speeding up the worsening of conditions such as arthritis, chronic pain, and diabetes. There is also evidence that the continued release of adrenal hormones eventually leads to the depletion of these hormones, which can exacerbate depression and anxiety. Chronic stress can also lead to increased muscle tension and fatigue, migraine headaches, ulcers, and irritable bowel syndrome (IBS).

Nearly every system in the body can be damaged by chronic stress. Stress-triggered changes can increase problems with respiratory conditions such as asthma, bronchitis, as well as susceptibility to colds and flu resulting from a decreased immune system.

In addition, stress may suppress the reproductive systems, for example, by altering menstruation and ovulation in women, triggering impotency in men, and precipitating loss of libido in both men and women. Reduction of insulin levels caused by chronic stress can contribute to adult onset diabetes.

To reiterate, chronic stress contributes to adrenal fatigue and exhaustion, and as mentioned earlier, our 24/7 pace year-round, is a major factor in burnout, exhaustion, and insomnia. The cumulative effects of chronic stress can totally overwhelm the system if effective strategies for managing are not sought out.

Chronic Stress and Physical Disorders

While the effects of stress come in several manifestations, we will first explore the physical. In Western science, stress is looked upon as increasing "wear and tear" on the physical body. People who suffer from chronic stress experience the manifestations in different ways, such as hair falling out, acne, teeth grinding, and weight gain or loss.

When we experience long periods of chronic stress, our immune system can be greatly compromised. I reiterate this because the immune system is so important in so many areas relating to our health. Coronary heart disease, migraine headaches, and asthma are negatively affected by chronic stress. As we examine these physiological factors more closely and how they can manifest into illness and disease, we will see how stress can be a major contributor to these conditions.

It is no doubt that our life span is increasing. In the year 2020, eighteen percent of us will be over the age of sixty-five. In our youth-fixated Western culture, our challenge is to get to a place where we believe our lives are as fulfilling now as they were in youth. How many in our Western culture live each day to its fullest, being the absolute best they can be? Do they know how to be fully alive or do they feel there is nothing creative or exciting left? They have to know that old age can be just as wonderful as youth, perhaps even better, depending on our attitudes. In Eastern cultures, the young and the old are all a part of the family. Elders are honored and revered, rather than looked upon as old and useless.

According to Harvard Health Publications, major life events and physical problems cause stress as people age. A constant state of chronic stress in addition to aging-related stress can damage the immune, endocrine, and nervous systems. Stress has been linked to many leading causes of death, such as heart disease and cancer, and can be considered as much a risk factor for disease as smoking, alcohol and drug abuse, overeating, or lack of exercise. Maladaptive coping to stressful situations can very often lead to an increase in these risky behaviors, thus raising risk even more.

Research shows that the speed at which you age is influenced by how well you manage your stress.

A Valued Teacher

Best-selling author, professor, global workshop leader, and award nominee for his documentary, *Earth Songs*, Brian Luke Seaward, Ph.D., has been a master teacher whom I have had the pleasure of knowing for nearly fifteen years, and from whom I have learned so much. He has written over a dozen books on managing stress, and understanding the nature of stress and the human spirit. Dr. Seaward's wisdom and knowledge have inspired many people and brought valuable insight for effectively managing stress in our modern culture.

Constance Clancy-Fisher, EdD

According to Dr. Seaward, stress and its effect on the immune and nervous system can lead to the conditions mentioned below:

Stress and Immune System Disorders

Colds and Influenza. When the immune system is suppressed, you are more susceptible to catching the common cold or the flu.

Gastric and Duodenal Ulcers. It has long been known that ulcers of the upper gastrointestinal tract are related to stress. More recently it has been shown that in most cases a specific bacterium is also involved. Such ulcers result from an interaction between stress and infection. People take antacids or antibiotics, but if the stress is not dealt with, their effects can be lessened.

Allergies. Perhaps one would not think that stress contributes to allergies; however, under stress, the body releases high amounts of histamine into the bloodstream, increases the adrenal gland's production of cortisol, and directs the nervous system to make more epinephrine and norepinephrine. An oversupply of these hormones lessens the immune system's effectiveness. Just thinking about a foreign substance (pollen, dust) and becoming anxious about it can set off an allergic reaction.

Cancer. Most cancerous tumors take many years to develop. Stress hormones tend to suppress the immune system and contribute to this illness, which continues to affect one out of every three Americans in some form. I have seen many women suffer from some traumatic event on an emotional level and succumb to breast cancer. I am not saying that stress causes cancer, but as the immune system is suppressed, some cells evolve into cancerous tumors.

Rheumatoid Arthritis. This connective tissue and joint disease results when synovial membrane tissue becomes inflamed. This synovial fluid may enter cartilage and bone tissue causing deterioration of the affected joints. The severity of pain is related to episodes of stress, including suppressed anger.

STRESS AND NERVOUS SYSTEM DISORDERS

Tension and Migraine Headaches. Tension headaches are produced by contractions of the muscles of the forehead, eyes, neck and jaw. When the contraction of these muscles increase, there is increased pain.

Migraine headaches are a more severe form of headache. This vascular headache includes symptoms of intense dizziness and nausea and is often described as being preceded by a flash of intense light. These types of headaches can be related to an emotional issue such as the inability to express anger.

Coronary Heart Disease. An increase in blood pressure may be related to stress hormones and is a risk factor for coronary heart disease. Over time the heart enlarges to handle the increased blood pressure, which is also called "hypertension." Hypertension can also lead to atherosclerosis, which in turn, increases risk of heart attack. A heart attack, or myocardial infarction, can lead to death or chronic heart failure, which over time results in death.

Irritable Bowel Syndrome (IBS). This condition can follow chronic bouts of abdominal cramping, pain, nausea, constipation, and diarrhea. The hypothalamus which controls appetite regulation is also associated with emotional regulation. No surprise that IBS is thought to be closely related to stress.

Bronchial Asthma. Secretion of bronchial fluids can precipitate an inflammation of the smooth muscle tissue of the bronchioles, resulting in bronchial asthma. The onset of asthmatic attacks can be associated with anxiety.

Temporomandibular Joint Dysfunction (TMJD). Excessive

contraction of the jaw muscles (teeth grinding/bruxism), which generally occurs during sleep, can lead to TMJD. Like rheumatoid arthritis and tension or migraine headaches, this condition is also associated emotionally with the inability to express feelings of anger.

I totally agree with Dr. Seaward's assessment. I hear countless stories daily from clients, friends, and family about the "migraine headaches" they experience after a stressful event, or IBS that paralyzes them and keeps them from enjoying activities.

Most, if not all of us, know someone suffering from a form of cancer or have lost a loved one to cancer. We are all too familiar with the manifestations of a stress-related condition.

STRESS AND ITS ANGER COMPONENT

"Anger is a result of people
Not acting the way we think they
Ought to act."

ROBERT FISHER, D.C.

Anger is a very primitive emotion. We tend to internalize anger, one issue on top of another until we cannot internalize anymore. Then we explode like a volcano, very often in response to some little irritation that triggers an explosive release way beyond what the actual issue would merit. Anger can be expressed in a variety of ways: hostility, frustration, passive-aggressive behavior, intimidation, intolerance, indignation, rage, bias, and prejudice. Severe angry outbursts can even lead to heart disease and stroke. Anger results from expectations that were not met to our satisfaction. Think about it, we all have expectations. We put demands on ourselves and others. When those expectations are unmet, we are angry, angry at ourselves and others. What could have been done differently? How could I have been so stupid? How could he be so thoughtless? If you are experiencing anger, this feeling may be a result of unmet expectations that you have. You can help yourself by monitoring all of your expectations and trying to determine what internal need of yours is being projected onto another. Are you a caregiver or pleaser? If you are, and you know who you are, then you are a master at giving away pieces of yourself for a payoff you anticipate. This is all about operating from the ego, and the feeling of gratification is often very short. Pay attention to your expectations and how you can better manage them. Below, I have included author Neil Clark Warren's valuable work on anger styles.

Note the styles and recognize any that seem familiar to you or someone you know.

1. The somatizer: This person is best described as someone who does not express anger. Instead, it gets suppressed and manifests in emotional and physical symptoms.

In time, the body takes its toll and these unexpressed emotions carry a heavy price.

Just some of the physical ailments related to suppressed emotions are TMJD, ulcers, migraine headaches, hypertension, liver problems, and rheumatoid arthritis. Women tend to have this condition more than men.

2. The self-punisher: This is the person who feels guilty about feeling angry and tends to punish the self with obsessive-compulsive behaviors. This may manifest in the form of excessive eating, drinking, shopping, gambling, exercise and sex.

3. The exploder: The exploder utilizes anger mainly through intimidation. This mismanaged anger tends to manifest in road rage, acts of violence, explosive behaviors, hostility, foul language and abuse. This behavior is more common in men, although it is exhibited in women as well.

4. The Underhander: This type of person will seek revenge in a perceived socially acceptable behavior, especially in a work setting. Passive-aggressive behavior and acts of sarcasm (anger) are forms of underhanded behavior.

People who use these forms of anger don't consciously realize that they are really giving their power away since the anger controls them. If you see yourself as exhibiting one of the above mismanaged anger styles, then the following exercise may help you learn to recognize and manage your anger in a way that will work in your favor rather than against it.

EXERCISE:

MANAGING YOUR ANGER IN A HEALTHY WAY

1. Can you select your mismanaged anger style from the list above? If so, what is it?

_____

_____

_____

_____

2. Pay attention to your anger and ways you monitor it. At the end

of the day, write down the events that caused you to become angry. Estimate the number of times you felt angry.

_____

_____

_____

_____

3. Learn ways to de-escalate your anger, (e.g., breathe and count to ten, exercise, walk away from the situation that is contributing to your anger, talk about it, write about it). Write down how you de-escalated.

_____

_____

_____

_____

4. Identify something you are angry about. List several things you can do to lessen the anger and write down how you can rise above it.

_____

_____

_____

_____

5. Define a situation that angered you and write down the

expectation that was not met. Now shift that expectation so it becomes more realistic and acceptable.

_____

_____

_____

_____

6. Forgiveness is a way to let go of anger and heal yourself. Write down the top three persons who you think have angered you and begin to take steps to forgive so you can move on and let it go.

_____

_____

_____

Psychological Components of Stress

THE TRICKS OUR MIND (EGO) PLAY

How often do you hear that inner voice saying, *It's just awful, horrible, terrible,* or *I should have studied more for that test. Isn't the economy just awful?*

I should never have eaten that hot fudge sundae. The list of the *should's, musts, oughts* continue to the point that we do not recognize what our thoughts are telling us. The late Albert Ellis, Ph.D., founder of the Rational Emotive Institute has written extensively on the irrational beliefs we all have at times and how to reframe them (See inventory below).

"Horribilizing" is the anxious anticipation of the possibility of a negative event. When we hear the phrase *what if?* as in these innermost thoughts: What if I miss the flight? What if I gain more weight? What if my relationship ends? What if I lose my job? What if our planet is destroyed? We get caught up in the what if mentality. Far too much of our energy is then spent wasted in "horribilizing" when it is more to our benefit to conserve energy rather than waste it on negative projections. *What ifs* tend to create havoc and chaos. They are prime examples of thought that is often irrational. As Dr. Ellis taught, the more you *should, must,* and *what if* on yourself, the more stressed you become.

EXERCISE:

HOW RATIONAL IS MY THINKING? LEARN
TIPS TO DISPUTE HORRIBLIZING

Through Rational Emotive Therapy (RET)

Take the following quiz to determine how rational or irrational your thinking is, Mark A or B as it applies to you.

1. A: I *have* to be loved and approved of.

    B: It is not possible to be loved and approved of by everyone. Since we are unique human beings we will connect with some better than with others.

2. A: I *should* always be competent, adequate, and perfect in all endeavors.

    B: It is neither necessary nor possible to always be competent, adequate and/ or perfect. Perfection doesn't exist. We each possess certain skills that are above average and some will never be highly developed. This is okay.

3. A: Some people are *bad* and *wrong,* therefore they *should* be punished.

    B: Only behaviors are bad and can be separated from the person. There is no bad person.

4. A: It is *awful* and *terrible* when things don't go the way I want them to.

    B: If things don't go the way I want them to, it is not that big of a deal. It may be a bit frustrating at the most.

5. A: Unhappiness is *external* and I *cannot* control it (unless I control the other person).

    B: Unhappiness is internal and I can control it regardless of what the other person does. I can be unhappy for the length of time and to the degree that I choose.

6. A: My early childhood experiences must continue to control me and determine my emotions and behavior.

   B: My early childhood experiences may have helped me form certain emotional or behavioral habits. However, I can choose to form new habits and ways of responding now.

7. A: There is invariably one right, precise, perfect solution and it would be terrible if the perfect solution were not found.

   B: There is never just one right, precise, or perfect solution. There are good points and bad points to every solution.

8. A: I *should* become upset over my and other people's problems or behaviors.

   B: I need not choose to become upset over other people's problems or behaviors.

9. A: The world *should* be fair and just.

   B: The world and the people in it are not necessarily fair and just. I will not triumph unless I actively stand up for my rights and what I believe in.

You can probably guess the irrational statements in the above quiz. If you answered A to some of the statements, you are thinking in an irrational way. If you answered B, then your thinking is rational. We all have an "inner committee," that internal critic who talks in a harsh, judgmental, self-deprecating way. You can listen to this condescending and judgmental parental voice, which offers no viable solution, or you can be your own best coach, and like any good coach, you can constructively seek understanding and awareness of the sources of irrational thinking and look for helpful suggestions for changing to rational thinking. By shifting irrational thinking into rational thinking, you can eliminate fears and catastrophic thoughts. When you think catastrophically, you anticipate the worst possible outcome accompanied by the worst consequences. Naturally, this creates unnecessary stress.

Thoughtful examination of these statements will speed you on your way to breaking the thought-stress syndrome:

EXERCISE:

REFRAMING STRESSFUL SITUATIONS

1. Describe a situation or event when you catastrophized and created stress and tension.

_____

_____

_____

_____

2. How can you reframe this situation to view it as positive?

_____

_____

_____

_____

3. What action plan could be implemented to improve the situation?

_____

_____

_____

_____

4. What are your natural strengths and gifts that can be applied to this situation?

_____

_____

_____

_____

5. Describe how you can maximize your natural strengths to reduce and eliminate catastrophizing in the future.

_____

_____

_____

_____

NOTE: Remind yourself to stay focused on the present. You have nothing to lose and everything to gain by staying right here in this moment. It is when we begin to think about the future that our anxiety develops. This in turn can result in catastrophic thinking. All we have is now.

Be your own inner champion, listen in a positive, encouraging, and constructive way to information that comes to you. Choose to be your own best friend. Use constructive rather than destructive criticism.

Take responsibility for your actions and view mistakes only as learning experiences from which growth can occur.

Women, Hormones and Chronic Stress

As a therapist, I am all too familiar with women trying to be the heroine of their own lives. Today's modern woman is exhausted, mentally, physically, emotionally and spiritually from living in a vigilant state of fight or flight. I witness women from 18 to 80 who live with an attitude of "I can handle this," only to discover that the body's resources have become depleted from overload. They end up with adrenal fatigue as a result of being chronically in the state of fight or flight, which often leads to insomnia, chronic fatigue syndrome, digestive issues, lowered immune function, depression, anxiety, and low libido. How a woman feels and functions is a strong indicator of her success and of her ability to accept and deal with what life presents. When I have an initial consultation with a woman, I take a thorough history of physical illness and disease. Then I begin to take a survey of the emotions she has been experiencing. What has meaning and purpose in her life? What makes her happy, unhappy?

Why is it so difficult for the average woman to admit that it is virtually impossible to be all things to everyone? Physically fit, beautiful, successful in her career and as a mother and wife. To say nothing of being highly sexual and sensual as well as forever young. Is it because that is what women were taught and what they are exposed to everyday on TV, and in magazines and other media? We need to realize that these are only the hopes and expectations of others who what us to behave the way *they* think we should behave and consume the goods and services they want to sell us.

Women tend to put others before themselves. They nurture others, and unconsciously, they want nurturing in return. When it is not reciprocated, there is a let down, a disappointment, another unmet expectation. If a woman is not nurturing herself, this sets up a dynamic for lack of healthy relationships with others. So for all of you women who are reading this, take note that you have an authentic self that has always been there. It just happened to get buried with all the day-to-day stuff. She is there waiting to emerge again.

If you have any of the symptoms mentioned earlier and you constantly feel overwhelmed and on overload, then speak to your doctor about having your adrenals checked. If you are suffering from adrenal fatigue, you have already set the stage for a compromised immune system, insulin resistance, hyper or hypotension and metabolic disturbances. It is essential you get proper nutritional counseling since diet is very important to improving your overall health. Proper exercise is another component of reducing the effects of stress as well as being a benefit to our bodies. Without proper monitoring of these health issues, women are at risk of allowing stress to make their physical issues worse.

In recent years we have heard a lot about bio-identical hormone replacement as being an alternative to traditional hormone replacement therapy (HRT). There is now a huge debate over the use of traditional Hormone Replacement Therapy (HRT). Because of the numerous side effects that have been experienced, and the data from the Women's Health Initiative showing an increased risk of heart attack and stroke, there is much confusion among women on how to proceed. Those who practice more holistically are proponents of plant-based sources of ingredients known as "sterols" that convert to female hormones to balance hormonal function. All women will have to educate themselves and work with their health care professionals to discuss what will best serve them throughout their developmental life stages.

Chronic stress has many physical manifestations as well as emotional, psychological and spiritual repercussions. Chronic stress can even affect the thyroid. When one suffers from chronic stress, the thyroid is overstimulated and eventually the thyroid hormones become depleted. Some common symptoms include hot flashes, constipation, insomnia, thinning hair, morning headaches, fatigue, depression and an increased cholesterol level. Excessive cortisol (the adrenal stress hormone) production can lead to loss of calcium which ultimately can lead to osteopenia and eventually osteoporosis. The body also compensates by limiting production of the sex hormones estrogen and testosterone, thus leading to a nation of women and men who do not feel the capacity or have the energy to enjoy a healthy sexual relationship. As Dr. Mehmet Oz reports, we are not getting enough sexual pleasure in our society. Both men and women are not having enough sex. When one has healthy stress levels, excessive levels of cortisol are stabilized and we are better balanced on all levels. Our cholesterol levels, liver function, and blood pressure all affect our physical health. So when the body is fed properly and exercised (physically, mentally, and spiritually), all systems are go and your body will reward you appropriately.

THE POSITIVE BENEFITS OF STRESS MANAGEMENT AND HYPNOSIS

Best-selling author, Ob/Gyn Dr. Christiane Northrup is a leading expert in women's health and wellness. She states that the way to help women of all ages achieve vibrant health is by "teaching them to tap into their inner wisdom, necessary to experience joy and fulfillment throughout life."

Happy people, we know through research, lead the most fulfilled lives. Studies have been done in cultures where people have longer life spans than in our culture. These cultures have strong family ties, a strong spiritual life, and trusted friendships, which lead to much lower rates of depression and anxiety. These people live life with meaning and purpose and remain active throughout their lives. Mind-body health, therefore, is about living your life in a way that makes you feel content, joyful, and connected with others.

People from cultures with long life spans prioritize family and create strong relationships that are meaningful. Research has shown that older couples who have healthy relationships and are healthy enough to have sex at least two times a week, live longer and have much more satisfaction in life. What is really interesting is that they look about ten or more years younger.

We are quick to see how the aging process is changing in our culture. The media have given us a profile of how someone *should* look, especially women, at a certain age. Entertainment Tonight (a popular TV show) informs us about how all the beautiful people maintain their youthful looks and can make average people think they need to run to a plastic surgeon and undergo every procedure known to man. Also, with so many anti-aging products and treatments on the market, people are continually encouraged to look younger.

What I am suggesting here, and what research shows us, is that nurturing ourselves and our relationships can contribute to a more youthful look, genetics being equal. As is accepted among many women today, we are not our grandmothers or our mothers. Now 60 is the new 40, and 50 the new 30.

CHAPTER TWO

Let's Get To Work To Manage Our Stress

"Through the power of my own
Thoughts, I can remove tension,
And stress and replace it with peace
And inspiration."

ANOMYNOUS

OBSERVING YOUR SYMPTOMS

WHEN YOU BEGIN TO BE aware of your stress symptomology, you will begin a healing process by determining which healing method is appropriate for what you are experiencing. Let's begin with the following list of physical, emotional, behavioral, and spiritual symptoms that stress exacerbates (this is only a sampling). We will examine work and home stressors, assessment of marriage and family, and once the self-inventory is completed, discussion of helpful hints will follow.

Place a check next to the symptoms that you have experienced within the last twelve months and list any others that you think are appropriate.

PHYSICAL

Cardiovascular system _____Coronary artery disease
_____Stroke
_____Hypertension
_____Arrhythmia
_____Other

Respiratory _____Asthma
_____Allergies
_____Sinus Infection
_____Other

Lowered Immune Function _____Lowered resistance to disease
_____Chronic Fatigue
_____ Brain Fog
_____Other

Autoimmune Disorders _____Rheumatoid arthritis
_____Inflammatory diseases of connective tissue and muscles (for example, fibromyalgia)
_____Other

Gastrointestinal disturbances _____Irritable bowel syndrome
_____Ulcers
_____Colitis
_____Gastric Reflux
_____Loose bowels or constipation

Genitourinary disturbance _____Impotence

_____Menstrual problems

_____Diureses

_____Frigidity

Dermatological disease _____Neurodermatitus

_____Acne

_____Rashes

_____Eczema

_____Psoriasis

_____Other

Emotional

_____Excessive worry

_____Tearfulness

_____Irritability or edginess

_____Depression

_____Obsessive thought

_____Frustration

_____Anxiety, fear, panic

_____Powerlessness

_____Lack of concentration

_____Lack of self-confidence/esteem

_____Loneliness

_____Impatience

_____Irrational anger

_____Other

Behavioral

_____Change in appetite

_____Aggressiveness

_____Change in sleep pattern
_____Daydreaming
_____Change in sexual functioning
_____Passive behavior
_____Road rage
_____Abseentism
_____Obsessive-compulsive behavior
_____Nail Biting
_____Change in personal appearance
_____Poor posture
_____Avoidance toward others
_____Anger toward others
_____Decline in productivity
_____ Hair pulling
_____Other
_____Teeth grinding

Spiritual

_____Little or no role for spirituality in my life
_____Wavering faith
_____Little or no use of prayer or affirmation as a healing tool
_____Rare attendance at any form of spiritual service
_____Rare or no periods of meditation or introspection

When you peruse a list like the one above, acknowledging the symptoms of which stress can be a part, be mindful that these symptoms did not emerge overnight. They won't magically disappear. It requires effort, dedication and help from your health care professional when necessary along with self work.

Work and Home Stressors
Stressors at Work

_____Job changes (role expands or decreases)

_____Increase of job demands

_____Expectations from others too high

_____Expectations for self too high

_____Change in status

_____Change in income

_____Administrative problems

_____Employee problems

_____Poor work relationships

_____Threatened Security

_____Other

Symptoms at Work

_____Projection of anger towards co-workers

_____Poor job performance due to preoccupation

_____Lack of interest in work

_____Need for support from others at work

_____Late hours and habitual overworking

_____Use of drugs or alcohol

_____Sleep on the job

_____Avoidance of time at home

_____Other

Home Stressors

_____Marital problems

_____Family problems

_____Problems in the family life cycle (separation, divorce, death, new baby)

_____Avoidance and/or isolation from family

_____Lack of emotional support from family members

_____High stress and tension in the home

_____Conflict and arguments

_____Poor communication

_____Other

Stress Symptoms at Home

_____Avoidance and isolation

_____Poor communication

_____Failure to attend to daily work

_____Use of drugs or alcohol

_____Increased anger with family members

_____Projection of own anger onto family

_____Excessive vacation and/or trips out of town

_____Other

Assessment of Marriage and Family

The following statements are an assessment of your marriage and family status.

Circle the response which best fits you. Then read the scoring key that follows.

1. I look forward to going home at the end of the day.

Yes   No   Sometimes

2. I feel supported by my spouse in my daily work.

Yes   No   Sometimes

3. My partner and I agree about our goals.

    Yes   No   Sometimes

4. My partner listens to my issues and concerns.

    Yes   No   Sometimes

5. My partner does not complain that I am not spending enough time with him/her.

    Yes   No   Sometimes

6. My children and I spend quality time together.

    Yes   No   Sometimes

7. There is mutual respect within our family.

    Yes   No   Sometimes

8. Am involved with family events.

    Yes   No   Sometimes

9. I feel challenged by my partner in a healthy way.

    Yes   No   Sometimes

10. My children have no behavioral problems

    Yes   No   Sometimes

11. My family is happy.

    Yes   No   Sometimes

12. My family feels that my work does not interfere.

    Yes   No   Sometimes

13. Arguments within the family are infrequent.

    Yes   No   Sometimes

14. My family does not try to get my attention in a negative way.

    Yes   No   Sometimes

15. I am attentive to my family's issues.

    Yes   No   Sometimes

If you marked eight to ten responses affirmatively you have a few marital concerns.

Five to seven affirmative responses indicate moderate marital issues, while four or fewer affirmative responses may indicate more problematic marital issues.

Respond to the following items about the stressors you're experiencing.

Describe the actual event that made you feel stressed.

_____

_____

_____

_____

_____

_____

_____

_____

_____

_____

_____

Constance Clancy-Fisher, EdD

Describe your reaction to the stressors regarding:

a) Your thoughts

_____

_____

b) Your feelings

_____

_____

c) Your behavior

_____

_____

d) Your fears

_____

_____

Did you tell anyone?

How are you choosing to handle the situation now?_____Is there any more you could be doing to resolve the stressful event?

_____

_____

What are you choosing not to do to resolve the stressor?

_____

_____

Why?

_____

_____

What unfinished business is contributing to your stress?

_____

_____

What do you think it will take to complete the unfinished business?

_____

_____

Now that you have an even greater awareness of how you're handling each stressor, check below what you think applies to you since they may be affecting actions you may be taking to resolve the stressful event.

_____Lack of confidence

_____Unclear expectations

_____Lack of support

_____Procrastination

_____Dislike of competition or excessive focus on competition

_____Unhealthy environment

_____Lack of emotional control

Pay close attention to these items. They may lead to maladaptive behaviors regarding the stressors you are experiencing.

If you checked lack of confidence, here are some suggestions to help you. Go to your favorite bookstore and look over books on how to develop self-confidence; read those that call to you. Once you have identified specific areas where you lack confidence, you may want to seek counsel with a professional to explore these areas and learn what you can do about them. Consider accepting yourself and your circumstances as they are at the moment. We are all human and we all make mistakes. Our challenge is to learn from mistakes, not repeat them. You also may want to list what you think your strengths are. We all arrive on this earth with special gifts and uniqueness. As you become aware of these gifts, and use them, you will achieve a sense of accomplishment and a greater level of self-confidence. Practice gratitude for all you have. It will add to your feelings of inner peace. Using your strengths to help others will reinforce and encourage your growth in a positive direction. You can make a difference in your life by helping others. It feels good to give, and such feelings and behavior will reinforce that you are a positive force in the Universe. Take time daily to look at yourself in the mirror and repeat "Every day in every way I get better and better." The more you do this, the better you will feel. Know your attributes and remind yourself of them often. These suggested tools and exercises will help boost your self-confidence.

If you checked unclear expectations, begin with clarifying your expectations as best you can. If this is challenging for you, perhaps you could speak with a trusted friend or advisor who could assist you.

If you checked lack of support, ask yourself if and how much and what type of support is really necessary for you to manage your challenges and accomplish what you are looking to achieve. There are family, professional, and community support systems available for practical and moral support when you are in need of emotional, social, spiritual, financial, medical, or legal help. You may want to consider attending a support group that deals with the type of support you need.

If you checked procrastination, ask yourself what you are trying to avoid and why. Procrastination is about resistance to making a change. We don't like change. We like to keep things the way they are because we feel more comfortable dealing with the known. Perhaps you are anticipating that making changes and new beginnings are too uncomfortable, or you lack self-confidence to make the change necessary. Think of something you did that you thought was going to be difficult and you were glad you did it after the fact. Some procrastinate out of fear that they won't achieve their desired goal.

Others cannot face making changes that seem overwhelming to them. Ask yourself what is overwhelming you. Assess the changes that need to be made, break them down into small steps, thus creating a realistic plan to achieve your goals. Strive to do the best you can and know that the outcome does not have to be perfect. Tell yourself you are doing the best you can with the knowledge you have at present. At the end of each day reward yourself for your perseverance.

If you checked dislike of competition or excessive focus on competition ask yourself, Do I need to compete or is there a possible win-win situation? If I need to compete, I will make sure that my actions are fair to myself and others. Is there a way to do the best that I can do without alienating others? Can I be a good example to others?

Very often being over competitive results from inner feelings of lack of self-worth.

If you checked unhealthy environment, what is it that feels unhealthy to you in your environment? For example, do you live in an unsafe area? Do other members of your family do things that make you uncomfortable, such as overconsumption of alcohol, smoking around you, stealing from you or others, using illegal drugs and encouraging you to do so? Is there a lack of educational opportunities? Talk with those you trust and respect and get their advice on how they would deal with the problems you face. See if this helps you think of ways to begin your transition into a healthier environment.

If you checked lack of emotional control, ask yourself if you regret actions you took after losing emotional control, such as physical violence toward another, uncalled for verbal abuse, harming one's self, behavior leading to loss of employment, and so on. If so, seek immediate therapy from a qualified professional. Therapeutic services are available in most communities at no charge through city or county social services.

External Stressors

External stressors are events that we did not see coming, such as accidents, unexpected illness, sudden loss of a loved one, the closing of our place of employment, among others. Since the majority of external stressors cannot be avoided, we need to find the help necessary to heal and to move on.

When Unexpected Loss Occurs

Our generation grew up with a parent or grandparent who lived through the Great Depression. There were many lessons to be learned from the experiences of that era. My great uncle told me stories about his life then. He bought his first stock when he was just nine years old. By the time he was 20, he was doing quite well in the market. Then the depression occurred, and he and others lost everything. He was very resilient and went right back to work and bought stock again. He built his portfolio again and did very well in the market for many years to come.

Our relatives were survivors in that era. They knew how to cope better than we do. They had realistic expectations, and they carried on. Yet the depression changed their lives. Many lost everything for which they had worked hard. The generations before us were no strangers to pain, physical, emotional, mental and spiritual, as many of us are experiencing now.

We as a society are now facing much of what these folks of the depression years faced. We were taught that if we did well in school, worked hard, went to college that we could have a great career, take a vacation annually and have a nice life. Many of us did all of those things yet still faced crises out of our control.

"You seldom sit at a crossroads and Know it is a crossroads."

ALEX RAFFE

Our lives are full of turning points and crises. So how does one begin to navigate through uncharted territory? Sometimes we have to grieve what was and learn to let go and accept what is to move forward. Grief is a part of life. We grieve not only what we have lost but also the hopes, dreams and plans that never were fulfilled. The late psychiatrist, Dr. Elisabeth Kubler-Ross, who was mainly known as one of the foremost authorities on the subject of death, dying and transition, identified the five stages of grief and their meaning:

1. **Denial**
2. **Anger**
3. **Bargaining**
4. **Depression**
5. **Acceptance**

Constance Clancy-Fisher, EdD

Denial is a conscious or unconscious refusal to accept what is, whether that is loss of a loved one, loss of employment, or loss of a relationship. It's a defense mechanism and perfectly natural. Some people can become locked in this stage when dealing with a traumatic change that can be ignored. Death, of course, is not particularly easy to avoid or evade indefinitely.

Anger can manifest in different ways. People dealing with emotional upset can be angry with themselves, and/or with others, especially those close to them. Knowing this helps one to remain detached and non-judgmental when experiencing the anger of someone who is very upset.

Bargaining is an attempt to avoid consequences. For people facing death, that can involve attempting to bargain with whatever God the person believes in. People facing less serious trauma may seek to negotiate a compromise. For example, "Can we still be friends?" when facing a break up. Bargaining rarely provides a sustainable solution, especially if it's a matter of life or death.

Depression is referred to as preparatory grieving. This stage means different things depending on whom it involves. It is acceptance with emotional attachment. It's natural to feel sadness and regret, fear, and uncertainty. Reaching this stage shows that the person has at least begun to accept the reality.

Acceptance, the final stage, indicates that a person has attained objectivity and some emotional detachment. Again this stage definitely varies according to the person's situation. People dying can enter this stage a long time before the people they leave behind, who must necessarily pass through their own individual stages of dealing with the grief. (Based on the grief cycle in *On Death and Dying*, Elisabeth-Kubler-Ross, 1969. Interpretation by Alan Chapman 2006-2009.)

"If we could see that everything, even tragedy, is a
Gift in disguise, we would then find the best way
To nourish the soul."

ELISABETH KUBLER-ROSS

"As in any journey, there is risk; any deepening of
Character necessitates a loss.
Nonetheless, initiating such a journey remains a
Watershed, an outpouring of anticipated grace
And indelible opportunity to drink from the deep
Well of your life."

SAKI SANTORELLI

My Thoughts on the Stages of Grief

Many different kinds of loss can initiate stages of grief. These stages are intertwined, and it is natural to weave in and out of different stages at any moment. I say to many of my grieving clients that grief is a strange thing. One moment we can think that we have it all together, then the next we literally fall apart. People ask me how they can "get over" the pain of grieving. Truthfully, the only way to get past grief is to go through it. There is no right or wrong way to grieve. You grieve in your own way.

One does not "get over" the losses of a loved one, a beloved pet, a job, a house, a marriage, a missed opportunity, a financial loss. Rather one heals through the grieving process and moves on. When grief strikes, go through it and realize that it is not the time it takes to grieve, but rather what we do within that time to heal that really matters.

Denial is our chief defense. It protects us from pain. If we

Constance Clancy-Fisher, EdD

block the trauma, then we don't have to work through the pain. The long-term consequences can be devastating, since we are not fully living, rather just existing from day to day with no relief from the pain. Once you can come to terms with denial, you will most likely be able to move into the next stage of grief. Remember, grieving is healing, as are the other stages, especially when you are able to move fully through each stage and come to acceptance.

For a time, anger is very often a part of the healing process. If we stay stuck in our anger too long, be it anger at ourselves, God, or a loved one, we obstruct the healing process. Anger makes our ego feel better, but not the soul. When aligned with the will of the soul, we want to open up again to living fully and wholly. When we support our ego, by expressing anger, we prevent ourselves from feeling true peace. Anger masks the real hurt that lies beneath the grief. Again, staying in anger too long can consume and immobilize you, which prevents you from healing the deep wounds at your core.

To work on letting go of your anger, journal about your anger. Then make a ritual of releasing or getting rid of your anger. You can bury what you journaled, or burn it. Tear the pages into pieces and flush them down the toilet. Pack them in a hot air balloon. Put them in a bottle and throw them out to sea, or throw them off a mountain top. Depression is a familiar place we go when we experience a loss. It is sad to lose someone or something we cherish and missed opportunities can engender regret. I remember hearing Christopher Reeve give a talk about five months before his passing. He said that he allowed himself to be depressed for ten minutes each day, then he went about his day. That was all, ten minutes.

Depression occurs along with the grief process. It passes. You weave in and out. If the depression lasts longer than a month, it is best to talk with your health care professional for information to help guide you through this difficult time. Talking with your doctor is the first important step in deciding the most appropriate treatment plan. People who suffer with long-term chronic depression, are at risk for heart disease and poor physical health. When you are in the throws of depression, it seems at times there is no way out. Know that there is and remember that it takes time to heal. When you are experiencing depression, you may lose your passion for living. Your symptoms may include a sense of helplessness or hopelessness, sleep disturbance, change in appetite, lack of interest in things that were once pleasurable, and a change in mood. People with a diagnosis of severe depression may have to be on an anti-depressant medication for a period of time. Medication can be prescribed by a medical doctor or nurse practitioner with experience in treating depression. Along with medical care, the assistance of a psychotherapist or psychologist can be most beneficial.

The rate of depression is on the rise from the number of women now trying to do it all, thinking they need anti-depressants to "get through the day." For these women it is easier to take a pill than to go to a therapist and seek assistance to make the necessary changes to overcome their depression. These women should be aware of the root cause of the problem that led to the depression, then make changes to resolve it rather than medicate it.

Acceptance is a place we reach when we have truly worked through the other grief stages and we are ready to move on. In acceptance we start to become aware of new opportunities, which may lead to new beginnings.

We have lived many chapters of our lives and there are more to come. We have come through a powerful life transformation, realizing that endings are inevitable, an essential part of the growth process. Endings always lead to new beginnings. Had we not reached acceptance, we would never have experienced this awakening and further growth would be delayed. Acceptance leads the way to become joyful again.

Constance Clancy-Fisher, EdD

"Acceptance means: for now, this is what this
Situation, this moment requires me to do, and
So I do it willingly. If you can neither enjoy nor
Bring acceptance to what you do--stop."

ECKHART TOLLE

WHAT ABOUT FINANCIAL STRESS?

Financial stress has always existed, and it is especially prevalent now with the current condition of our economic times. Individuals who at one time never thought they would face the conditions prevalent today are dealing with high levels of stress. Lenders were encouraging us to borrow money to buy that bigger house, take that much needed vacation, pay for our children's college education, and so on. Now many are in the kind of debt that cannot be repaid in their lifetime. Why did this happen?

We were taught and encouraged to continually want more: the fancy car, the huge home, the designer labels, and the finest of everything. This is the "I'll be happy when syndrome," which leads to temporary satisfaction, not authentic happiness. On the island where I live only a few little charming cottages remain. Most were torn down and replaced with trophy homes. I once asked a friend of mine, who was a builder, why people had to build such huge homes. He had a quick response, as if it were a no brainer, saying, "because they have seven other homes just like this one." It is what they know. Yes, the known and familiar. If they had the money to invest in property, they did. Today, many of these so called trophy homes are sitting empty, and some are even in foreclosure.

Financial stress brings with it intense levels of fear. Television news programs that focus on the woes of the economy, featuring economic experts who warn of recession leading to depression and interviews with Americans who face an uncertain future help to spread a culture of fear. According to a recent poll of Americans between the ages of 44 and 75, 61% said that running out of money was their greatest fear. The other 39% said that death was more frightening.

Living in fear can ultimately lead to health issues. As mentioned earlier, while the effects of stress and fear come in several manifestations, there is increasing "wear and tear" on the physical body. People who suffer from intense fear experience unhealthy manifestations in different ways, such as hair falling out, acne, teeth grinding, and weight gain or loss. When we experience long periods of fear, our immune system can be greatly compromised leading to illness and disease.

For most Americans, the time has come to learn to live with less, especially fewer material goods and less stuff, most of which ends up in our closets and garages. If you are a child of the 50's and 60's, chances are you have accumulated so much that you don't know where to begin to let it go. A friend of mine who has not worn something in over six months donates it to a charity. She uses the saying, "when in doubt, throw it out." Seek a financial planner to assist you with your financial goals. It is more important than ever to face your financial future realistically. You want to create lasting abundance, and if you are the one who knows you need help, reach out and get help! Write down your beliefs about money, then divide the list into two categories. In the first, list the beliefs that are favorable toward money; in the second, outline the beliefs that are not favorable, especially the ones in which money is seen as evil or difficult to get. Try to remember where these negative beliefs came from and then release them, realizing they interfere with and inhibit the achievement of your financial goals. Abundance will flow when you have an understanding of the energy of money. If you can learn to manage money, you will feel secure on all levels. Always have gratitude for all that you do have.

We know now more than ever that what is held in the mind expands. Focusing on a negative thought gives more energy to that thought and is more apt to bring it to fruition. The same thing is true of a positive thought. This makes the choice easy. Do not let doubt creep into your consciousness. If it begins to appear, picture yourself hitting the delete button. Do it right away and repeat this exercise if the doubt presents again. Do your best to catch and dispose of doubt immediately.

TECHNO STRESS

As I mentioned in the introduction, we are living in an era of techno stress. I wrote about this in my first book twelve years ago. Today we seem to be plugged in more than ever since we now live in a global society where what happens in one country affects another. I recently saw on a news report that employees are never getting away from work since they are connected to their office via blackberries or other techno devices, and they are sick and tired of having no down time. It's as though they are in a perpetual state of working, never really leaving the office. One employer, finally realizing the downside of constant pressure on his employees, told his employees that they can turn on their "out of office" reply on their computer at 5:30 p.m. each day and they did not have to turn it off until 8:30 a.m. the next morning. The same goes for cell phones and other devices. These employees can now have a life outside of work. Unfortunately, this is rare.

However, we are now finally beginning to see a backlash after over a decade of rapidly increasing technology. While technology was supposed to make our lives easier, it is doing quite the opposite, this rapid increase of techno stress is overwhelming people with its constant demands, leading to an increase in illness and disease, addiction, depression and anxiety.

A colleague of mine was in a cafe last year, and he was astonished at what he observed. There were four adolescents sitting in a booth. In over fifteen minutes, he never saw one of them look up and talk with one another. They were all buried in their techno devices texting. He said he just sat there in amazement watching them. All he could think of was that we have we lost our humanness.

Interviews with my clients lead me to believe the majority of people are not coping well with the loss of social interaction, which is being replaced more and more by the increased use of techno devices. Do families spend quality time with each other? No, they don't. Now more than ever according to a Nielsen poll, reported in its "Three Screen Report" (referring to televisions, computers and cell phones), the average American now watches more than 151 hours of television a month. Teens watch about 6 1/2 hours of video on a mobile phone per month, as opposed to the nearly three hours that adults ages 18-24 watch. Internet usage overall grew 3.6 percent from the same time a year ago, to 27 hours a month. There is also an increase in the number of electronic devices in households.

We need to return to family quality time. Quality family time can include visits to a park or museum, walking or hiking, and picnicking. At the same time all family members need to have a period of quiet time for reflection and meditation so a healthy balance can occur.

Remember the days when Sunday was sacred? Stores were closed. That was the day families gathered for noon meals and outings. We need to return to that simplicity. A time when life was more balanced and far less stressful. So the next time you are tempted to go to the mall on a Sunday or surf the Internet all day, think about spending quality time with loved ones instead. You will be glad you did.

GEOGRAPHICAL/ENVIRONMENTAL STRESS

Geographical stress refers to specific stress related to or affected by environmental change. Is there any environment that constitutes a stress-free environment? A small town, resort living, mountain life, rural country living? While there are certain places that are more conducive to less stressful living, every locality can experience unexpected hurricanes, earthquakes, droughts, floods,

Constance Clancy-Fisher, EdD

and wildfires. For example, during the first nine months of 2012 much of the United States experienced the hottest temperatures on record according to a CNN report. The United States had the warmest spring since record-keeping began in 1895. According to a recent article in the Washington Post, this has been the eighth-warmest year globally on record. Wildfires in the United States this year consumed the second-largest number of acres since records began in the 1960's, topped only by 2006. The Mid-west experienced the biggest drought in half a century. In October 2012, hurricane Sandy, fueled in part by warmer-than-usual temperatures flooded the coastal areas of New Jersey and New York City, destroying hundreds of homes. There is no way of predicting what we may be exposed to. We need to choose to live our lives in ways that give us enjoyment. Worry and fear of events we have no control over produce unnecessary stress. There is no way to avoid unexpected events.

If you happen to live in an environment you believe to be constantly contributing to your stress levels, here are some thoughts and tools to modify your environment to lessen stress:

1. If you live in a big city, plan a weekend getaway to a place that is calm and tranquil. Many beautiful places that can be wonderful escapes are not too far from major cities.

2. At home or at work take a moment to use guided imagery to help with stress reactivity. Imagine that you are relaxing in a peaceful place that brings soothing comfort. Use your senses to see, feel, hear, smell and really notice the beauty surrounding you. Peaceful imagery can make your current environment seem more tolerable.

3. Familiarize yourself with the ancient art of Feng Shui. This Eastern way of creating peace and harmony with nature and your environment is one way to feel more harmonious with your surroundings. Feng Shui invites chi or energy, into your

home or workplace so you can feel a sense of relaxation and positive energy.

4. Practice healthy living strategies to reduce the harshness of your environment.

   For example, if the conditions are unpleasant outdoors, join a fitness center and exercise indoors. Take a buddy along to participate in outdoor activities you both enjoy.

5. If you live in a high crime area, invest in an alarm system or attempt to move to a neighborhood that has a security watch or to a gated community since these are usually safer. Have a neighborhood meeting to create an emergency phone relay system to notify each other of any unusual activity. Establish friendships with neighbors and cultivate additional ways to make your area more safe.

"There's a quiet place I know where nature sings to me the Music of the mountains and the forest and the sea. It is not Far away, and it sometimes seems a place removed from Daily life, a distant dream of time and space. I have been Lost in city streets, in traffic fast and loud, where sirens Scream and nature's voice is drowned out by the crowd. And so I go to seek that place where I become a part of Nature's song-that quiet place I've found within my heart."

PAUL CONRAD

Constance Clancy-Fisher, EdD

THE EFFECTS OF STRESS ON CHILDREN

"Chronic patterns of self-hate, guilt, and self-
Criticism raise the body's stress levels and
Weaken the immune system."

LOUISE HAY

Children are sensitive to others' thoughts and moods. Therefore, it is no surprise that they pick up on their parents' stress and the stress of others with whom they are in contact. Just as stress in adults originates from many different sources, the same is true for children. Babies are alert and sensitive to the world, even in the womb before birth. The messages they receive from those around them shape their emotions and beliefs. Studies suggest that babies who are separated from their mothers too soon after birth(even when there is a medical problem) are at greater risk of emotional problems later on. A significant bond between mother and infant is essential. Wounds that don't heal from infancy and childhood, such as episodes of isolation, abuse, and abandonment, whether children are conscious of them or not, go with them into adulthood. These wounds don't heal, but persist. During my years as a teacher, guidance counselor, and therapist, I observed many children who suffered from stress due to various traumatic emotional situations, such as divorce, addiction, depression, anxiety and post traumatic stress disorder (PTSD). Negative programming is another issue children face.

Often it is not maliciously intended, for example, "Jon, you are so bad for leaving your dirty clothes on the floor." "Mary, how could you be so stupid"? Negative programming, from an adult thrust onto a child, can be internalized into *I'm inadequate, unworthy, or bad*. These feelings become influential components that lessen self-esteem. Because of the intense effects that traumatic emotional issues and negative programming have on children, they are capable of carrying these wounds into adulthood. Very often they become part of the walking wounded, which unfortunately is so prevalent in our society.

Our society needs to teach children to focus on the positive rather than the negative. It is a universal law that what we focus our energy on expands. This is true at any age.

It is just as easy to be positive as it is to be negative when we realize the damage that focusing on the negative can do. Teach children to focus on their strengths rather than their non-strengths and to keep their expectations realistic. When reaching out to our children, encourage them to share their feelings, especially if they are sad or melancholy. Ask them to share how their day in school went, and always help them to see the positive. Art therapy, self-expression through writing, drawing, painting, sculpting, is a beautiful way to encourage expression of emotions. With the prevalence of dysfunction in many families, children need guidance counselors who can spend quality time with them encouraging expression of their feelings and emotions. Children need to be taught early on how to increase self-awareness and self-esteem, as well as learn methods to handle stress effectively.

EXERCISE FOR CHILDREN AND ADOLESCENTS

The following exercise is for children and adolescents to help reduce their stress levels.

1. List people, places, things that contribute to your feeling angry, resentful, depressed or anxious. (Parents, explain the meaning of certain words to your children that they may not know):

    _____

    _____

    _____

    _____

    _____

    _____

2. What do you do when you feel this way?

    _____

    _____

    _____

    _____

    _____

    _____

3. What are other things you could do when you feel this way rather than what you normally do?

    _____

_____

_____

_____

_____

_____

4. What do you do to make yourself feel better?

_____

_____

_____

_____

_____

5. Who can you go to for help and support?

_____

_____

_____

_____

_____

Constance Clancy-Fisher, EdD

Children are wonderful candidates for hypnosis because they have not been subjected to the amount of mental conditioning that adults have. They are trusting and open to the process. See the index for information on relaxation, guided imagery, and meditation for children to help reduce stress.

DEALING WITH ANNOYANCES

Whether it's the big stuff or the small stuff, it's all stuff. It is easy to get frustrated with our day-to-day trials and tests that can be ever so small yet still drive us crazy. Some of our interactions with others can seem so senseless, but still have to be dealt with. Take my friend Gwen, for instance.

Gwen and her husband were walking on the beach one morning with their two dogs. They had been walking on the same beach for a couple of months. Suddenly, a police officer sped toward them on his little beach four-wheeler and told them he was giving them a citation because their dogs were not on leashes.

"What"? Gwen exclaimed, "Yes they are on leashes." (In truth, they were not holding them all the time.)

"You are not in control of your dogs," the officer responded.

Gwen said, "There is no one here."

The officer went on to say, "It doesn't matter, you are breaking the law." Well, her feisty combative spirit took over, and an unpleasant encounter became even more so. They received a citation.

Afterward, Gwen asked herself what lesson she could learn. She realized that if she had shown the officer respect and kindness, knowing he was doing what he was instructed to do and explaining her side of the story calmly, he probably would have given her just a warning and asked her not to do it again.

Sometimes when annoyances linger, we start looking for ways to feel better.

We seem to think that we will be happier when certain external circumstances work in our favor.

Do any of these statements sound familiar?

I'll be happy when...

+ I lose 10 pounds
+ I get out of this relationship
+ I get that job
+ My boss gives me a raise
+ I get that promotion
+ My hair is straight
+ It gets cooler
+ It gets warmer
+ I get a tan
+ I get a cat
+ I get a dog
+ I take that long awaited vacation
+ I get the new car
+ I get the house I have been wanting
+ I get the diamond ring
+ I can get out of this town
+ I go to the concert

If any of the above statements resonate with you, ask yourself if you were really happy when you received what you desired. Maybe you were, but was the feeling temporary? Usually it is. External "fixes" work for the ego but not the soul. Soul growth comes from inside your authentic self. We have become a society of immediate gratification seekers which leads to momentary happiness until the next want presents itself. I want this and that, and it will all be good and I will be so happy and satisfied. The temporary high. Then reality sets in: external things bring fleeting happiness. Real and lasting happiness comes from within.

Constance Clancy-Fisher, EdD

Physical, Emotional and Spiritual Health Management

There are many ways to learn skills to reduce stress and improve your quality of life. In today's techno stress world we have lost our way and become too caught up in the "24/7" lifestyle that ultimately has or will affect our physical, mental, emotional and spiritual health. As you begin to navigate your way by working from the inside out rather than the outside in (the American way of "I'll be happy when"), you will begin to achieve greater happiness by becoming aware of the person you were born to be before society programmed into you the cultural aspects of how you *should* be and act. Happiness and joy come from within, something we all need to realize and incorporate into our way of being.

Better Nutrition and Its Contribution toward Optimal Health

Better nutrition aids us in healing the physical effects of stress and reaching optimal physical well-being. I am not a nutritionist or dietitian, yet I am aware of the grave concerns regarding the effects of a poor diet and its contribution to poor overall health.

Depleted Adrenal Glands and Continuing Chronic Stress Can Be Associated with High Sugar Diets

We might not think that a high-sugar diet can be the result of a stressful condition, but this may sometimes be the case. Acute stressors may trigger a surge of powerful biochemical processes in the body. It starts with the adrenal glands. The adrenals produce many different hormones. When the initial stressor is underway, they begin by producing adrenaline. The adrenaline surge prepares the body to be ready for *fight or flight*. This is a short-term response.

With the increase of adrenaline, you have that increased short-term strength (some people have lifted a car to get someone out of danger). Later, cortisol is produced. Cortisol is the hormone that helps subdue the initial adrenaline rush after the crisis has passed. If you have an ongoing stressor that becomes chronic, however, the levels of adrenaline and therefore cortisol remain high longer than they should. Gradually the adrenals may become depleted, but if the chronic stress remains, the body may then in some people crave sugar for the energy that our depleted adrenals can no longer regulate.

Let's look at what may be the diet of a chronically stressed individual.

Breakfast: Sweetened coffee, bowl of sugar-coated cereal or pastry, sweet drink or juice. Some people skip breakfast completely.

Lunch: If you are on the go or you eat at your desk, lunch may look something like this: Chips and soda, instant soup or a burger. If you are really super busy, maybe you skip lunch or munch a candy bar.

Dinner: Are you the king or queen of take out? Pizza and diet soda? Burger and fries? Half gallon of ice cream with chocolate sauce? On the nights you are too tired to stop by the take out place do you settle for cheese and crackers or a bowl of sugar-coated cereal? If you regularly eat foods of the typical American diet as outlined above, you are feeding your body in an unhealthy and eventually harmful way. The problems with such a diet in general are of two kinds, quality and quantity. Daily intake of foods high in sugar and fat with little nutritional content does not support the body qualitatively, since the body needs protein, vitamins, minerals, and some carbohydrates to support metabolic processes. Quantitatively, fat is more than twice as rich in calories than either protein or carbohydrates, and the body requires some fat but less

Constance Clancy-Fisher, EdD

than protein and carbohydrates. In addition and very important, eating too much of any food, that is, in amounts greater than the energy you expend, leads to overweight and obesity. Obesity is defined not only as weighing too much for your height (body mass index of 30 or higher) but also as having too high a percentage of fat in the body, a combination that leads to many other illnesses, such as type II or adult-onset diabetes, cardiovascular disease, and some cancers as well. Today, obesity affects people of all ages, including children, and is considered to be epidemic in the United States and in other developed nations. Obesity has pushed the incidence of type II diabetes to levels unheard of before in our country, leading to the development of this type of diabetes in children and calling for a new name to designate what was once called "adult-onset diabetes."

Focus on Eating as a Part of a Healthy Lifestyle. Balance in eating is as important as balance in relationships and other aspects of life. Instead of adopting limiting attitudes toward eating, such as, "I need to diet to reduce my weight," think of eating as nourishment for the body, the temple of your spirit on earth, and experience for the soul's growth. To safeguard your body by reducing risks associated with lifestyle, learn about and adopt eating habits that enhance health. Eat protein in moderation as well as starches. Avoid fatty and fried foods. Remember the advice your mother gave you to eat your vegetables. Don't forget fruit and nuts (in moderation) as nutritious contributions to your overall health. If you have been told you are at low risk for cardiovascular disease, eat eggs in moderation. Organic eggs are nutritious, but they do contain levels of cholesterol (dietary cholesterol) that may increase levels of cholesterol in the bloodstream and may have other effects as well, such as triggering allergic reactions in people so inclined. Look for healthy protein shakes that include nutritious ingredients.

Always read labels on everything you buy. Many products contain unhealthy levels of fat, sugar and sodium that do not contribute to a healthy lifestyle. Buy organic products if your food budget permits. Check out the website of the Environmental Working Group, which has created a shopper's guide that rates fruits and vegetables from least to most contaminated, with recommendations on the foods that should always be bought from organic producers if you want to reduce exposure to pesticides and herbicides. You can go to http://www.ewg.org/release/when-should-you-buy-organic.

A few suggestions from Bob Fisher, D.C., on proper food combining:

1. When you eat protein, don't combine it with carbohydrates. Always combine protein
   with vegetables which are low on the glycemic index.
2. When eating carbohydrates combine them with vegetables that are also low on the glycemic index.
3. Fruits should be eaten by themselves.
   Eating this way aids in stabilizing your blood sugar levels. Eat enough so that you feel satisfied. If you don't eat enough, your body will feel hungry usually within an hour or two after eating. If you overeat, your body will feel sluggish and sleepy.

   + Eat Foods that Enhance Good Feelings and Mood. Pay attention to the foods you ingest, do you feel good within the next few hours or are you sluggish and moody?

     If you are sluggish and moody, you will now know which foods to avoid. If you feel good, you may want to eat more foods that made you feel better. Being aware of how certain foods make us feel may help us to become more mindful of how other situations in our life make us feel.

Constance Clancy-Fisher, EdD

- Abstain from Sugar Substitutes. Sugar substitutes, such as aspartame, alias Nutra Sweet, Splenda, Equal, and others, in diet sodas and other low fat products, do not reduce sugar cravings; studies show they increase them. Stevia is a natural alternative to the artificial sweeteners listed above. Read labels. Many popular and well-marketed products have little to no nutritional value. Consult with a nutritionist or dietitian for information on diet and eating habits that will make you healthier and, if you are overweight, aid you in achieving more optimal weight.
- Establish a Healthy Support System. If you go out to eat with family or friends, tell them about your new dietary guidelines so that they will not encourage you to eat unwisely. Ask for their support as you tell them how serious you are about your lifestyle change. Allow no one to sabotage your efforts.
- Practice Taking the Utmost Care of Yourself. You are worth it. I tell my clients this all the time. Commitment to a healthy lifestyle will help you feel good about yourself.

Practice self-care on a regular basis to foster health in mind, body, and spirit. You are whole, and your wholeness thrives on integrating all three of these components. You live in your body. Take care of it and it will take care of you.

"A lot of the time our state of mind (if it is negative) will result in sending messages to the body to crave certain foods (usually unhealthy) to maintain that state of mind. So changing your state of mind (becoming more positive) can result in our body's calling for foods (most times more healthy) to maintain a more desired state of mind."

BOB FISHER, D.C.

Making healthy food choices is an integral part of a healthy lifestyle. The best medicine is prevention.The diet that has been getting rave reviews for years and is well researched is the *Mediterranean Diet*. This diet is based on the diets of people who live in Italy, Spain, Greece and other Mediterranean countries and is high in vegetables, fruits, whole grains, nuts, fish, olive oil and includes a modest intake of wine. The guidelines recommend limited intake of dairy products and meat and no trans or saturated fats from processed food. The diet features fish that contain omega 3 fatty acids which are important in many of our bodily functions, such as keeping blood from clotting, maintaining the fluidity of cell membranes, lowering the amount of lipids (fats such as cholesterol and triglycerides) circulating in the bloodstream, and helping to prevent cancer cell growth. The use of olive and canola oils, which are high in mono- unsaturated fats, is encouraged. Studies have shown that people who have made this diet a permanent lifestyle change live longer and healthier lives and have lower incidence of heart attacks, diabetes and cancer. There also is evidence of a slowing of age-related cognitive impairment in people who eat this way.

Weight Loss and Maintaining It

No one diet works for everyone. I recommend the Mediterranean Diet because it is very easy to incorporate as a part of permanent lifestyle changes. Exercise is one of the keys to weight loss. If you are overweight, proper diet and exercise will go a long way toward helping you lose weight and keep it off. My experience has shown that hypnosis for weight loss seems to be effective for people who really desire to change their behavior. The most important tool in weight loss and maintaining it is a positive self-image. I have worked with hundreds of patients who wanted to lose weight. They were successful in not only losing the weight but also keeping it off. They had to be deprogrammed of old core beliefs and reprogrammed with a new positive belief system that enhances self-image. Negative old beliefs can be like toxins in the body that need to be removed.

I record the sessions so that the patient can replay them, continually reinforcing the positive new programming. Positive mind-body connections enhance a positive self-image, which aids in achieving success in whatever we do. An interesting side note regarding weight loss: My husband, Robert H. Fisher, D.C., has helped many of his patients who were overweight. Many returned to their normal weight for their height and body type. A number of their histories revealed that they began to gain weight at a time when events occurring in their lives were creating moderate to severe stress, especially times of lack of feeling loved and appreciated, or lack of resources especially of a financial nature. It seemed that their bodies responded to the stresses by storing more adipose tissue. Fear of lack seemed to be felt by the body as well as the mind. When he would make them aware of this coincidence and they would work with the mental as well as the physical aspects, the result was the weight loss they desired.

Affirmations That Encourage Healthy Eating and Weight Maintenance

- I am mindfully aware of the healthy food choices I have everyday.
- I choose to select only the best nutritional foods that are conducive for maintaining a healthy weight.
- I am comfortable with the variety of foods I have to add to my diet.
- I am educating myself on the best combinations of foods to eat and I will continue on this path.
- I allow myself to weigh and be aware of the appropriate weight that is best for my body.
- I allow my healthy eating to influence my slender and toned body.

Proper Emotional Management and Its Contribution to Optimal Health

People with healthy emotional balance maintain low levels of stress, worry and conflict. They are able to play and have fun, and create purpose in their lives. They actively develop and nurture relationships. However, as obsessed as we are about looking good in our culture, we neglect to take the best care of ourselves. We are good about buying ig houses and cars and eating at fine dining establishments, shopping at malls that seem to be everywhere, and striving to be the looking good family. Look at our role models: underweight osteoporotic women who set the standards in the fashion industry.

Psychoneuroimmunology (PNI) is the field of medicine that deals with the influence of emotional states as stress and nervous system activity on immune function, especially related to the onset and progression of disease. Negative emotions such as anger, guilt, resentment and grief, when prolonged, can affect the type of chemicals that are produced by the brain. This alteration can negatively alter nervous system function activity thereby lowering immune system function in our bodies. Minimizing stress can help minimize our risk of certain types of cancer, Alzheimer's and numerous other diseases. The choices you make in your life about reducing stress, eating well, exercising and having positive relationships can add ten or more years to life expectancy. The average life expectancy for men is about 72 years; for women, it is a bit longer at 78 years.

Many illnesses are related to lifestyle. The human body ages more slowly and has less illness and disease when optimal living conditions are present. We can create those optimal conditions. We seem to maintain our automobiles better than our bodies. Many people who neglect to take care of themselves may end up in the hospital unnecessarily. While there are advances in modern medicine and technology that can help prolong life, there is nothing better than taking good care of yourself to prevent illness. Case in point. I knew a man in the 60's who lived the high life. He chain-smoked camel filter cigarettes; he drank Manhattans, about five or six per day; he partied hard. In the 1970's, when this man was in his 50's, he began not to feel well. His doctor told him he had to stop smoking and drinking, start a healthy diet and lose weight. He was an avid golfer and really did not exercise in other ways. As time went on he not only ended up getting a quadruple by-pass, but also years later he suffered a major stroke. He survived, with much rehabilitation. However, his life and his health continued to deteriorate. Why did he smoke, abuse alcohol, party too much? He used them as coping mechanisms for stress. This man chose to continue to live the lifestyle that contributed heavily to the cause of his poor health.

People who sustain a healthy lifestyle find much fulfillment in their later years. What is it worth to you? You might be thinking that you know someone who chain-smoked and drank and lived to be in their 90's. Yes, there are exceptions, but few. It would be better to start healthy and stay healthy. Do not wait until you have your first health crisis or some other type of wake up call. I see that too many times in my counseling practice. Very seldom do people come to me pre-crisis to work on learning proper stress management. They are usually already in crisis and desperate for help. For example, they've been told to stop smoking. I ask if they *want* to stop smoking, and often they look at me as if I were crazy. They really don't want to stop; rather they were told they have to quit for health reasons. I am hesitant to take the case of a person who truly does not want to make the necessary *change* for improving his or her health. To be successful, people truly have to want to change and release current behavior. When someone really does not want to make a change, it will not be effective.

THE ROLE OF EXERCISE

Physical fitness is an important part of achieving optimal health. It makes you feel better and adds to self-esteem. This is very important in a culture where many people don't seem concerned about their health, but gradually more of us will want to look and feel better. Exercise plays an important role toward weight loss. Most people who exercise regularly maintain a normal weight. Exercise helps you to feel alert, more focused, and alive. It aids digestion, increases muscle mass, helps prevent osteoporosis, improves your libido, and helps you sleep better. Have you ever noticed that people who enjoy exercise look happier and younger? There is no one exercise plan that fits all. If you like to jog, then jog. Some people prefer a fitness center while others enjoy the outdoors. If you are someone who is not self-motivated, get an exercise buddy or exercise with a group. Recreation centers have many classes that are fun and provide great exercise, such as a spin class, aerobics, pilates, and water aerobics. Make sure you do plenty of stretching before and after any exercise. Remember that the most important thing is to exercise regularly. Be sure to check with your health professional before starting any exercise regimen. If you prefer to exercise at home, you can purchase a treadmill or an elliptical trainer. There are many DVDs of different exercise regimens available. A word to the wise, start slowly. You want to like exercising and not get so sore that you decide to quit. Again, it is finding the optimal exercise that works for you.

I am fortunate that I like to exercise. I don't always like a hard core workout, but enjoy the outdoors and being in nature. Personally, if I had to choose a favorite form of exercise, it would be hiking. There is something so freeing about being out in nature, and it makes me feel good. I hike with my dogs, and they enjoy it as much as I do. We can all find our niche.

If you have not exercised in a few days and you feel the desire to get out and move, you are well on your way to a new lifestyle. If you are uncertain where to begin, it might be worth the investment to hire a personal trainer to get started. It can be motivational because you are committing to an actual appointment and learning how to work with your body in a safe effective way.

Affirmations to Consider with Exercise
+ I allow myself to exercise to keep my body slender, healthy and fit.
+ I allow myself to be attracted to the exercises that are best for me.
+ I allow myself to enjoy a regular exercise routine.
+ I allow myself to easily achieve and maintain my ideal body weight.

A WORD ON HERBAL MEDICINES

"Herbs are the "Millennial Medicines"
They have been around forever and
Will be here forever."

MARK BLUMENTHAL

Herbs have been successfully used as healing remedies in many cultures throughout the world for thousands of years. Medicinal plants have been sought worldwide and taken to treat a wide variety of illnesses, such as anxiety, depression, dementia, and insomnia. According to the *Alternative Medicine Newsletter,* the use of complimentary and alternative medicine in the United States continues to expand. This growth can easily be seen in the current use of herbs and supplements. The six most popular selling herbs are ginko biloba, St. John's wart, ginseng, garlic, echinacea, and saw palmetto. Consultation with a health practitioner before taking herbs and supplements is always recommended in order to avoid adverse side effects and drug interactions.

WESTERN/EUROPEAN HERBS

Some of the more popular herbs include:
1. Chamomile is thought to have a mild sedative effect. This is often taken in the form of tea.
2. Evening primrose is thought to reduce hyperactivity in children.
3. Garlic acts as an antioxidant and has many beneficial uses such as treating age-related memory loss, to lowering blood pressure and preventing strokes.
4. Ginkgo biloba is thought to improve blood circulation, improve memory, and may be useful to relieve the symptoms of Alzheimer's disease.

Constance Clancy-Fisher, EdD

5. Ginseng is one of the world's most famous herbs, often referred to as an "adaptogen," a relatively new term for substances that increase the body's overall resistance to all types of stress. Proponents of ginseng claim it increases energy and endurance, and has some anxiolytic effect.

6. Lavender consists of essential oils, with over 100 compounds. It is used by herbalists for relaxation from nervous tension, restlessness, depression and insomnia.

7. Lemon Balm is a member of the mint family that is used to relieve anxiety and insomnia. As an inhalant, lemon balm is used as aroma therapy for Alzheimer's disease.

8. Valerian is thought to be an effective and reliable sleep aid. It is also claimed to be effective for reducing anxiety, nervous irritability and possibly depression. When combined with lemon balm it enhances sedation.

Note that in 5 percent of subjects, there may be a paradoxical stimulant effect.

TRADITIONAL CHINESE MEDICINE

Traditional Chinese Medicine (TCM) dates back thousands of years and is used by 25 percent of the world's population. The American Association of Oriental Medicine (AAOM) estimates that over 12 million Americans visit TCM practitioners each year.

AYRUVEDIC MEDICINE

Ayurveda is the ancient holistic Indian art of healing that has taken hold in our Western World. Ayurvedic herbs are said to increase energy, improve digestion, reduce symptoms of illness and reduce free radicals in the blood. One of the focuses is on purification of the body.

CHAPTER THREE

Embracing Necessary Changes With Less Stress

THE KEY TO SERENITY

"God grant me the serenity to accept the things
I cannot change, courage to change the things I
can, and the wisdom to know the difference."

REINHOLD NIEBUHR

WHY DO WE RESIST CHANGE? We resist change out of fear. This
is quite common. We fear the loss of the known. It is scary to
navigate without a map into uncharted territory.

We become quite accustomed to the known and familiar even
when it causes discomfort. People find it difficult to understand,
let alone comprehend, why battered and abused women remain in
abusive relationships rather than leave. Most of these victims have
been so beaten down that they remain in victim consciousness, and
they see no way out. They live in total fear, at times concerned for
their lives. Can they be helped? Yes, but it takes an experienced
professional to lead them back to where they need to be to return
to a normal life.

"Resistance is just another limiting
"Belief that we have manufactured to
Protect our other limiting beliefs."

"When there is no resistance there
Is simply "what is," and life flows
Naturally without obstruction with a
Natural feeling of well-being."

HALE DOWSKIN

When experiencing resistance to change, ask yourself whether your fears are a result of situations that occurred in the past and if they really have any relevance to the situations you are facing now. If we learn to open ourselves up to the grace of change, surrender what we need to relinquish and accept the new that follows, we will feel far less stress than if resisting change. One of my favorite things to do is view the full moon whether I am at the beach or in the mountains. Its magical beauty from fullness to tiny crescent sliver through the month is always a spectacular sight. I observed the moon last night with its cycle just over half full. The moon never really disappears from sight; it simply changes cycles as do our own lives. Change can add beautiful meaning and grace if we allow it to shine into our hearts as we welcome new beginnings.

CHANGE REQUIRES LETTING GO OF FEAR
AND SELF-LIMITING BELIEFS

EXERCISE

On Change

Describe the significant changes that have occurred in your life within the past two years.

_____

_____

_____

_____

_____

How did you respond to these changes?

_____

_____

_____

_____

How would you respond to those changes now?

_____

_____

_____

_____

Constance Clancy-Fisher, EdD

Truly, if we are resistant to change, we are resistant to growth. I remember when I was in college and then graduate school, taking doctoral classes, everyone sat in the same seat week after week. I always wondered why. They were not assigned seats, but people got used to that sort of comfort. Likewise many families like to vacation at the same place year after year, forgoing new adventures. Not that there is anything wrong with that; we just need to be aware of what we are doing.

In September 2011, my husband and I took a road trip from Colorado to Sedona, Arizona, to attend a lecture. We took a side trip to Moab and the Grand Canyon. As we looked down the canyon in awe, we saw risk takers walking and sitting literally at the edge of the cliff; one missed step and it would be all over. I am not saying you have to walk to the edge of the cliff literally, but symbolically, supposing your purpose in life is to be the best you can be. This requires growth, which very often includes the element of risk and requires facing change throughout your life. The longer you procrastinate making changes that are ultimately in your own best interest, the more difficult it will become. You will struggle even more when you have no choice other than to make the change. With the economic downturn, many homes on Sanibel Island decreased to half the value they once were. A friend of mine, Greg, decided to sell his house even though he would have to take a loss. His realtor had a potential buyer who was sure he wanted the house and had the financial means of purchasing it. His realtor was so sure of this sale, Greg went to the point of moving all of his belongings out of the house and donating much of them. As he told me, it felt good to donate to an organization that would pass his things to people who would benefit from their use. The buyer backed out at the last minute. Not only that, another potential buyer did the same thing months later. Were they afraid of change? Were they resistant to leaving their known and familiar environments and taking a risk? Greg kept hearing from the realtor how badly they "wanted this house," until the day the papers were to be signed. Buying or selling a home can be an emotional experience. It was especially emotional for Greg to let go of a home with all its memories and items that meant a lot to him. Eventually the house sold, but Greg wondered what fears made the two buyers back out on the day of closing and if they ever regretted not following through with their intention to purchase a wonderful piece of property. Greg had no choice but to sell his house, and he had to ccept what was inevitable anyway. We don't always understand the "why" of an event, especially if it seems like a negative or disappointing situation. We may feel anger, fear, helplessness and hopelessness, as if our life is never going to get any better. I believe all things happen for a reason, and that is a tough one to swallow. We all want to know right now just what that reason is. The reason isn't always available to us. If we accept that there is a greater good and there are forces working toward that greater good, we will be all right. Surrendering to our life's plan brings us to our highest good. Down the road we may have a greater understanding of the reasons why, but we may never know. This requires faith and patience. In Greg's case, he knew the Universe had its reasons for putting him in a situation where he had to sell his house. He told me he is aware that this unforeseen change will lead to more learning and growth and that his future will be all the better because of it.

"We can learn not to keep situations or events alive
In our minds, but to return our attention
Continuously to the pristine, timeless present
Moment rather than be caught up in mental
Movie making. Our very presence then becomes
Our identity, rather than our thoughts and emotions."

ECKHART TOLLE

A Word About Anxiety

For most people experiencing anxiety, you are out in the future worrying, fretting, stressing out about what might or might not happen. All of these emotions result from living outside present moment awareness. We all do it. We worry about the mundane, and we worry about circumstances that are out of our control. The mundane are situations we can do something about, for example, the laundry that didn't get finished, the taxes that have not been filed, the house that has yet to be cleaned this week, the studying that has yet to be done, the car that has yet to be washed. Examples of anxiety out of our control include: Is our country's economy going to remain in recession?

Am I ever going to earn enough money to pay my outstanding debts? Am I going to die of cancer? To manage anxiety, we have to stay in present moment awareness, and do what the present moment requires. Speculating and worrying about future events that may or may not happen is not productive and can lead to health consequences.

The Art of Meditation to Lessen Anxiety

The ancient Buddhist practice of *mindfulness* has become a part of mainstream America in the last couple of decades. The first hospital stress-reduction clinic, at the University of Massachusetts Medical Center in Worcester, Massachusetts, began in 1979, directed by Dr. Jon Kabat-Zinn.

Dr. Kabat-Zinn, mindfulness based stress reduction (MBSR) guru, has facilitated thousands of MBSR workshops for professionals and lay persons alike. MBSR is about letting the mind be as it is in the present moment. It is not about getting somewhere else. It is allowing yourself to be where you already are. Breathing mindfully is a simple remedy for reducing our ever-increasing levels of stress. The question I receive most often is "Can anybody meditate"? The answer is: yes, you can. Meditation involves intentionality. If you can breath, you can meditate. Meditation is not about feeling a certain way. It is contemplation and reflection. It is truly about moment-to-moment awareness. I tell students that the thoughts will come in, so let them. Just allow yourself to let them pass through.

Make a commitment to meditate and stick with it. You may start with sitting or lying down for at least five minutes, and just relaxing.

Make it a regular part of your life each day. When people say they can't meditate, what they are really saying is they won't make time for it. I was teaching a class years ago at the Vail Athletic Club one evening. We were just getting positioned and suddenly the door was flung open! "What is this class"? A woman asked loudly.

I said, "It is mindfulness meditation class. Would you like to join us?"

"I don't have time to meditate," she exclaimed as she ran away.

I feel sorry for those who think they have no time to meditate. Once someone experiences the positive changes that meditation brings to his or her life, he or she will always find time to meditate. How do you know when you are out of touch with the present moment? You might be thinking of other things like work while you are playing with your children. When you are in the shower, your mind is on dinner. When you are making love, you are thinking of other things you should be doing. While walking, you are oblivious to the beauty of a sunny day, because you are lost in thought and missing out on life in the moment. When you have problems, it is always easier to find solutions with a clear mind. Meditation increases clarity of mind and present moment awareness.

Constance Clancy-Fisher, EdD

Meditation is not only for emotional well-being. It is an excellent tool for lessening physical ailments and improving them. One of the physical benefits noted is a stronger immune system. One technique is being aware of one's sensations in the body and one's thoughts about those sensations. Here are a few examples of what students in the 8-week MBSR course had to say about their physical well-being:

+ "I was diagnosed with hypertension before the class and now my blood pressure is lower."

+ "I am an asthma sufferer and since I have been in the class, my asthma is under control."

+ "I suffer from chronic back pain, and I am in less pain now than I have been in years since I have started the course."

+ "I have suffered from migraine headaches for years, and now that I meditate every day I can honestly say that my migraines are less frequent. Maybe they will be totally gone with more meditation practice."

Kabat-Zinn teaches that through the practice of mindfulness meditation, you can learn to develop greater calmness, clarity and insight by embracing all of your life experiences, even all the trials, and turning them into occasions for learning and growth so your wisdom deepens and strengthens.

Some of the tools that you will begin to use and experience with MBSR are:

+ Reduce stress by responding mindfully rather than carelessly reacting

+ Access your own deep inner resources for learning, growing, and healing

+ Bring greater clarity to your daily life and everything you do

- Reduce or overcome addictive or self-destructive behavior patterns
- Enrich your experience of everyday living by being fully present in the moment

Mindfulness meditation is a way to develop a high degree of self-awareness in your life.

Practicing mindfulness can help us be aware of cause and effect. We begin to realize that if we react with anger that it returns in some way. If we express love and kindness, love and kindness returns to us. We gain more knowledge of how to create peace and harmony in our lives. Mindfulness can free you from being stuck in fear or uncertainty about the future (what many people are now experiencing) and assist you in living your life as an adventure one moment at a time.

"People are like stain-glassed windows.
They sparkle and shine when the sun is out,
But when darkness sets in, their true
Beauty is revealed only if there is a light
From within."

ELISABETH KUBLER-ROSS

LET'S GET STARTED PRACTICING MEDITATION

The first step is to find a quiet space. Get into a comfortable position that feels right for you. Be open and receptive to the thoughts coming in. Simply be aware of them without judgment or criticism and allow them to dissipate. This may take some time, so please be patient, and relax. Meditation is an acquired skill, the more time you commit to practice meditation, the more benefits

Constance Clancy-Fisher, EdD

you will receive. There is no good, bad, right or wrong way to meditate. It is simply your way.

In the mindfulness based stress reduction classes I led, a majority of the students had taken transcendental meditation (TM) back in the sixties and somehow gotten away from the practice of it. They were ready to begin again. Again, the practice of TM or any other form of meditation is designed to promote a greater sense of well-being and inner peace in both mind and body. Mindfulness can also be experienced while gardening, by focusing awareness of the true beauty of soil and the plants. Awareness grows through the practice of meditation, and we become mindful of everything we do. Remember the practice is about being in the present moment and fully experiencing where you are in that moment. No judging or criticizing, just being. In the mindfulness meditation classes I used to take my students for a walk outside, and they would come back with a new awareness of how beautiful nature truly is. There is really no set time for meditation; however, most people who meditate seem to enjoy the early morning.

Begin with a few minutes. Then as you become comfortable with meditation, increase your time to 20 to 30 minutes a day. You will find when meditation becomes a part of your daily routine and you skip it, you will miss it and return to it quickly. However long you meditate, be patient. It takes time to clear the clutter of thoughts from your mind. With increased practice you will find that meditation conveys a sense of peace and relaxation and may lead to an awareness of how much less stressed you feel.

ANOTHER FORM OF MEDITATION

It starts with the breath. In our fast-paced society, we often don't breathe as deeply as we should, especially if we are stressed or anxious. This slow, deep and focused method of breathing, also referred to as diaphragmatic breathing, is how infants breathe. This focused breathing has been a practice, especially in the Eastern cultures for centuries, to induce relaxation. This practice is also incorporated into other techniques such as hypnosis, guided imagery, progressive muscular relaxation, and autogenic training. Focused breathing is helpful for expectant mothers during labor, and is reported to reduce the pain of delivery. If it can be an effective tool for childbirth, then it can be effective for anyone experiencing pain.

Meditative breathing has two parts: inhalation and exhalation. When we inhale, the diaphragm contracts and pushes downwards, causing the abdominal muscles to relax and rise. When we exhale, our diaphragm relaxes, the abdominal muscles contract and air containing carbon dioxide is expelled.

EXERCISE:

1. Get into a comfortable position either sitting or lying down and close your eyes. Focus on your lower abdomen, by placing the palm of your hand there and begin to feel the belly expand as you slowly take in a deep breath. Slowly exhale, feel all your stress and tension and negative thought patterns releasing from your body.

2. Continue to repeat this breathing cycle. You should begin to feel your body relax as you follow your breath in and out. Continue for five to ten minutes and then observe how your body feels.

"When we go to a medicine person or healer because
We are feeling disheartened, dispirited, or depressed,
He or she might ask questions like, "When did you stop
Singing? When did you stop dancing? When did you
Stop being enchanted by stories? When did you begin
Finding discomfort in the sweet territory of silence?"

ANGELES ARRIEN

Getting Comfortable with Silence

Some people have a difficult time dealing with silence. I have had people from New York City stay in my home on Sanibel and they could not sleep because it was "too quiet." They are used to sirens, taxi horns, and other street noise. The opposite has happened to me. I have spent time in New York City and had difficulty sleeping because of the sirens, taxi horns and street noise.

When we do have the opportunity to really engage with silence, we have a chance to focus on the inner self rather than what is going on around us. Silence offers time for reflection and introspection, often allowing answers to unanswered questions to surface.

It is during silence that we can hear what the soul knows. I know that times when I am silent and there are no distractions, I often receive information that is invaluable to me.

Perhaps the reason that I was feeling stressed during the day becomes so clear that I have to laugh, and the laughter elicits in me a pleasant shift in consciousness. Revel in silence when you can. Listening to your higher self helps you to live on a more evolved level. This is a challenge for most of us; yet it can be achieved. Do not force anything. Relax into the moment. Silence is your friend.

"Follow your breathing, dwell mindfully on your steps
And soon you will find your balance. Visualize a tiger
Walking slowly, and you will find that your steps
Become as majestic as hers."

THICH NHAT HAHN

ALONE TIME

Some people think they don't spend enough time alone, while others think they are alone too much. What is alone time? Being at one with the activity you are doing without the distraction of other people or responsibilities. Make time for yourself. It may be a few hours to go into another room to read, write, or just be. Go for a walk or a bike ride. You may even need a weekend away in a private setting. Whatever works for you is fine. Alone time is a way to rest and rejuvenate.

Being single until age 53, I spent much time alone, yet I would make time for friends and family, and I felt I had a comfortable balance. Now that I am married, I am not alone as much. When I need alone time I walk on a beach, or hike in the mountains, or bike ride. This feeds my soul, and I like hanging out with myself from time to time.

"Your sacred space is where you can find yourself
Again and again."

JOSEPH CAMPBELL

Sacred Space

It may be helpful to create a sacred space. It should be in your own home in a special room or space where you can display items meaningful to you: photos, rocks, shells, religious objects, or art you have collected. Make your sacred space a place of comfort and peace. When you enter it, leave your cares outside. This is where you give thanks for all the good that life has given you. May your life's journey be full of sacred spaces and places.

CHAPTER FOUR

Positive Changes

"Here is a test to find whether your
Mission on earth is finished: If
You're alive, it isn't. "

RICHARD BACH

A POSITIVE MENTAL MIND SET

Believe it or not, it is just as easy to be positive as negative. There are optimists and pessimists in this world and there are givers and takers. Which are you? Optimists are those who live with the glass half full. They see the positive in the world and have an attitude of gratitude. They are the givers. Givers put others first; it is just a part of who they are. The development of one's attitudes, thoughts, and beliefs are formed early in life. Our attitudes and beliefs influence the outcomes of situations we face. Each situation just is. We make it good or bad by how we perceive it.

Negative thoughts and attitudes, just like positive ones, can become self-fulfilling prophecies in our lives. One's thoughts, beliefs, attitudes, and perceptions, are a powerful source of energy. Why not use this energy to create conditions in our lives that lead to peace and happiness?

Attitude is everything. How often do we stop to express gratitude to someone, whether it be a stranger or someone we know, for the kind acts they perform? Be grateful for the gift of life and the beautiful planet we live on. Be grateful for your loved ones, your home, your health, your joy. I remember one of the first hikes I took alone years ago. When I reached the top of the mountain and looked down at the tiny town below, I felt overwhelmingly grateful to be healthy enough to reach the top. There was no one to celebrate with or hug, yet I felt a powerful presence. I held out my arms, looked up to the sky and expressed gratitude that such an enchanting place existed.

A positive person mostly maintains a feeling of gratitude. Using the power of positive thoughts and attitudes in your life, being in the moment, using the breath meditation to breathe in relaxation and exhale any negative thought patterns, you can feel better through your day. You will have increased energy, be more in tune with yourself, and thrive. If you catch yourself with a negative thought, say to yourself STOP! Then reframe the negative thought into a positive statement. An example of this would be changing "I am so fat," to "I am grateful for the awareness that I can shift my body weight to a weight that I am comfortable with and is healthy for me."

When you say something that is negative, catch yourself in the middle of your sentence. Image yourself hitting the delete button or say, " I delete this thought." Then make a positive statement about what you truly want. You will be amazed at how easily you can change your negative thought to a positive one. Be grateful for all that is going right in your life. Remember that whatever you give energy to expands.

The Power of Positive Affirmation

Ever question the constant mental chatter of your ego? Psychologist *Carl Jung* referred to this constant mental chatter of the ego as "psychic tension." We all go there at times. There is a way to convert this "psychic tension" to positive affirmation. Jung referred to this as "psychic equilibrium." It is reprograming the tension by positively affirming a thought that releases the psychic tension. It is like changing the track on a CD from a song we don't like to one we do. It's switching from the ego to the essence of the soul. It does take practice and consistency in continually transforming negative thoughts to positive optimistic thoughts.

The following steps can guide you to this shift:
1. Become aware of your thoughts. When you are in a difficult situation, access the situation and what your thoughts were before the situation developed.
2. As you develop your awareness of these negative thought patterns, especially, in difficult situations, create a positive thought to replace the negative thought, and always give your energy to the positive thought. Focus on what you want.
3. Constantly remember, what you focus on expands. You attract into your life what you think most about. It only makes sense that when you choose to focus on something positive, the positive prevails. With your increased awareness, you should have a good sense of how to focus on what you want rather than what you don't want.
4. 4. Keep in mind that you are looking to raise your level of mindfulness, and thus your consciousness, to cultivate a positive mind frame that is with you all the time, during stressful times, especially the ones out of your control.
Compile a list of positive affirmations that appeal to you. Put the list somewhere you can see it, so that you are reading and saying your affirmations daily. If you start with "I" or "I am"

Constance Clancy-Fisher, EdD

or "I have" you are validating your affirmation. Always use the present tense as in "I have a beautiful loving spirit."

Before you know it, the affirmations you select will become a part of your daily self-talk. You will be repeating them quietly to yourself when you are driving or taking a shower, and especially when you lie down to go to sleep at night. The following are a list of affirmations to get you started if you don't already have some that you have incorporated:

- I am calm and peaceful.
- I have wonderful relationships in my life.
- I am beautiful inside and out.
- I am grateful for all my God given gifts.
- I am financially abundant.
- I am always kind and generous.
- I am spiritually alive.
- I am blessed to have so much in life.
- I am optimistic and positive in all situations.
- I love each day and live it to its fullest.
- I have optimal health.

HUMOR IS HEALING

"Fear is the lock and laughter's the key to Your heart."

CROSBY, STILLS AND NASH

Stress contributes to illness and disease. Good humor reduces the negative effects of stress. We have a choice: to live in fear and be unhappy or to live in love and be happy.

Live, laugh, love! When we practice all three to their fullest, we are celebrating each moment and the gift of life. In today's society, we all need a good laugh to keep our spirits in check. A sense of humor emerges when you accept things as they are. Enlightened souls (like the Dalai Lama) laugh often.

Norman Cousins, editor of *Saturday Evening review*, said: "Good spirits are a vital part of life. Denying joy is one of the greatest deprivations on this planet!" Cousins ought to know. He was faced with a serious degenerative condition. He began reading Dr. Hans Selye's *The Stress of Life* and examined what role his emotions played in his illness. He decided that love, hope, humor and laughter did have merit in the healing process. How did he come to this conclusion? Cousins watched classic episodes of the television show *Candid Camera*. He also spent 10 minutes of each day belly laughing. He discovered the joy of loosening up the abdomen and relaxing the solar plexus muscles. Cousins later wrote the book, *Anatomy of an Illness*. He mentioned that just "ten minutes of laughter allowed two hours of pain-free sleep." Can one literally laugh him or herself back to health? Why not? Laughter is truly healing. Physiologically speaking, it boosts your immune system and helps the brain release endorphins, which are natural pain relievers and mood lifters. Laughter increases immunity by increasing gamma interferon, which speeds up the production of new immune cells.

People who laugh release nervous energy built up from repressed thoughts. Famed psychiatrist, Sigmund Freud suggested that the act of laughter may release the stored energy of sexual and hostile impulses suppressed by the conscious mind. He believed the greater the suppression of thoughts, the greater the laughter needed to release them. In my stress management workshops I tell the participants to belt out a good belly laugh for at least 25 seconds. Not only is it good for reducing blood pressure, stimulating circulation, facilitating digestion, reducing tension, it is contagious. When someone in the room sees another person laughing, he starts

Constance Clancy-Fisher, EdD

laughing. Then in no time everyone is laughing. Laughter is also a great ice breaker and a wonderful way to release stress. Sometimes when we get so serious, we need to start laughing and be able to see that we get ourselves so uptight over the silliest things. The best time to revel in the humor is when we are at our wits end. Instead of BMWing (bitch, moan and whine) see the humor, it's a great alternative. Studies show that children laugh up to 400 times a day while adults may laugh a couple times a day. When we enter adulthood, most of us get caught up in the seriousness of life. We're tired, we're stressed, we're miserable and oh so serious. I ask participants in my seminars to write about the last time they remember having a good belly laugh. I encourage them to visualize the event; where they were, whom they were with, what triggered the laugh. At this point, the group is usually somber and quiet. I usually prod them with "Gee this is so serious!" A few people laugh. Then I have the group share their stories, and it only takes a few moments before everyone in the room is laughing and having fun. As the room lights up and everyone is happy and joyful, the participants realize how serious they were just before the exercise. They usually observe that the exercise was a great way to make them realize that they need to laugh everyday.

Our inner critic has been telling us for years that laughing is for kids. What happened? We left childhood and got serious. Perhaps you were told, "Stop being so childish. Quit being so silly. Stop laughing and get serious." Children are often stifled. Laughter is not just for kids. We all have a funny bone. It just needs to be tickled. Let's take the laughter exercise a step further: Return to your childhood and write about a funny experience. Perhaps you were watching a comedy show on TV. Maybe you were with friends or family when a funny thing happened. Now repeat this exercise recalling a time in adolescence when you found humor in a situation. Then go to your young adulthood and relive something that provoked laughter. When doing this exercise, we often realize that when we become adults, situations are not as funny. We need to resurrect the inner playful child. We all have an inner child who would just love to come out and play. Let that happen.

MY EPISODE OF LAUGHTER AT THE VATICAN

Years ago, I decided to accompany my dear friend Father Carmen Caruso on a group trip to Italy. I was single and living alone at the time and thought it would be a way to see Italy and not have to travel alone. While most of our journey was through Tuscany, we stopped at several villages and cities during our tour. While we were in Rome, we spent a day at the Vatican. It was a lovely fall day, and Pope John Paul II was to appear in his popemobile. Just as he was approaching, I noticed a group of nuns standing in front of Father Carmen and me. I asked the nun in front of me to please sit down so I could see. She turned around, and snapped "photo!" at me. I noticed she was taking a photo of the pope. I asked her again to please sit down so I could take a photo, too. She ignored me, so I tugged on her "flighty hat" and it fell off! She turned around and began yelling at me in Italian. Father Carmen said he could not believe I pulled her "flighty hat" off! Well, we started laughing and were in hysterics like two little kids. We could not stop. Humor presents itself in any situation if we just look for it. I realized after the whole scene that my buttons had been pushed. Having to cope with nuns was a trigger from my grade school years. My coping technique was laughter. What a beautiful way to get through a challenging time! This time around, I was in control, as opposed to my grade school days when nuns were controlling me.

It's ironic how a situation in my adult life turned out to be such a humorous ordeal at, of all places, the Vatican. Sometimes our inner child can come out to play in the most amusing ways. You don't have to wait for a special occasion or event in your life to enjoy your life and laugh.

Integrating humor into your daily life:
1. Look for the humor in what you experience. If you don't learn to laugh at yourself then how are you going to benefit from what laughter offers? Instead of being so serious, lighten up.
2. Watch comedy shows or films. Whether it's an old comedy movie or reruns of Seinfeld or Frazier, expect to crack up. A great way to boost the immune system!
3. Practice belly laughing everyday. Think about something really humorous and just start really laughing. The more ridiculous, the better. It will give your internal organs and muscles a fabulous workout! Try it for 30 seconds.
4. Start a comic relief notebook. Write anything or paste cartoons or photos in the notebook that put a smile on your face. Share the notebook with friends and ask them to start one. Share among yourselves. Before you know it, you will have a great collection of humorous sayings, stories, cartoons, and funny photos. Laughing makes you feel good inside.
5. See yourself as more than your work. Unless you are a comedian, you most likely need to be serious in the work that you do. We tend to forget that we are not all about work. Not that you should start taking your work less seriously, just take yourself more lightly.

As a therapist, I work with people on their concerns, grief, depression, divorce, addiction, and anxiety. I help clients begin to see the light in their darkness and emerge with some sense of hope and encouragement. When appropriate, I even encourage them to see some humor in how they react even in difficult situations.

I get them to understand that humor is good for the soul and encourages a cathartic release of emotions. Humor therapy is used in many therapeutic programs. Remember Patch Adams? He was the physician who dressed as a clown and made his primary healing method humor rather than medication with children in hospitals. Humor therapy is used in other rehabilitation programs, including the treatment of physical trauma and addiction. It has also been a stress reliever for the military. Remember the days when comedian Bob Hope traveled to visit the troops and had them in hysterics?

The Wisdom We Learn From Animals

"Many animals spend a lot of their time just sitting or Standing around. I think it's very likely that at some of This time they feel a sense of connection with the Whole."

MATTHEW FOX

There is a saying, that until you have loved an animal a part of your soul remains unawakened. Anyone who has an animal knows the joy and happiness that their unconditional love can bring. Animals are healers, too. They possess wisdom and insight that humans very often are not aware of.

I have always been an animal lover. I had cats growing up and when I was in my twenties, living in a condo in Houston, I wanted to move to a place where I could have a big dog and run on the beach. That dream came true. The breed of dog that best suited me was the Labrador Retriever. Labs were the best thing that happened to me from my thirties on. Those of you who are animal lovers can totally relate to my story. Pets give us comfort in difficult and challenging times. Our animals teach us so much,

Constance Clancy-Fisher, EdD

and it's up to us to pay attention and learn from their expression of unconditional love.

Specially trained therapy dogs assist the elderly in nursing facilities, retirement centers, and hospitals. Sometimes they are brought in to cheer up a terminally ill patient or someone who is recovering from a surgical procedure. Just the sight, touch, and connection between the patient and the animal has been known to heal a broken heart and lift one's spirits. Animals aid in de-stressing anxious college students, and home care facilities have reported seeing and hearing from the patients how good the therapy animal helped them feel. It is not that they remove stress, but they assist in calming down someone who is upset or anxious. Most people who own pets visit their physician less often than non-pet owners. So your pet may lower your health care cost.

"Things Fluctuate to Fit the Bill"

LUCAS CENTURY

Throughout our lives we learn many lessons related to work, relationships, and managing our time to make the best use of it.

APPLYING WHAT WE HAVE LEARNED

For those fortunate enough to have work, find something positive in your work setting and focus on it. Even if you are not happy in the current job, stay positive knowing that you will attract something better. There is a silver lining even though you don't see it just yet. Focus on what you have rather than what you don't have. As difficult as times are on this planet, this is an extraordinary time to be here. When you feel you need assistance, get it. Whether from a counselor, member of the clergy, or support group, help and support are available.

Our work is an extension of ourselves. When you put positive energy into your work, you will find that you are appreciated for what you do, your work environment is more supportive of your efforts, and your co-workers are more respectful and considerate. Make it a point to honor those with whom you work and treat them the way you wish to be treated.

Affirmations to Consider Regarding Your Work Life
- I allow myself to have a creative work environment that supports my endeavors.
- I allow myself to be happy and productive in my work.
- I receive an income that is perfect for my current situation.
- I have wonderful ideas that aid the growth of the company that employs me.
- I am willing to take risks for my own personal growth.

TIME MANAGEMENT

"Come out of the circle of time and
Into the circle of love."

JALAUDIN RUMI

When you analyze your daily schedule, create a to-do list and organize items from most important to least important. Doing the most important things reduces stress, allowing you to manage your time more effectively. The steps below will help keep you on track:
- Decide what is most important to you and the amount of time you want to spend on it.

Constance Clancy-Fisher, EdD

- Use a day-timer to help you stay organized.
- Plan ahead so you don't get caught up in feeling pressured with too many things to do. You may find that at times some things have to be put off.
- Practice deep breathing techniques to remain calm.
- Get a head start on your work day by picking out what you are going to wear the night before. If you take your lunch, make it ahead. Get a good night's sleep and leave early for work. Running late creates stress.
- Have a family meeting weekly to check in and offer assistance to anyone who needs it.
- Meditate to feel more peaceful and have more clarity of mind.
- Eat breakfast. You need energy to start your day. Keep it simple so preparation doesn't create stress.
- Take time at night to reflect on your day.

Realize that work can be joyful and relaxing when you use your time effectively. Approach each day, including your work days, with mindful awareness of staying present to the moment. When you are in the present moment, time seems to expand because you are not worrying about the future or the past.

"Fearlessness is the first prerequisite of a Spiritual life."

GANDHI

When I first started going out with my husband Bob, he told me, in a kind way, that I was "scattered." Well, that made no sense to me. I just didn't understand. Me, scattered? What on earth was he talking about? For the most part I thought I had it all together. I often commuted from the East Coast to the West Coast and worked out of cities in both areas. I was constantly running here and there, rushing from one task to another, checking e-mails and voice mail. I lived with an incessant hum of anxiety. Yet, I slept pretty well, ate healthy foods, and exercised. So what was the problem? It took a few months to process what Bob had observed. In fact, my life was scattered. I made the decision to resign from corporate work and return to my private counseling practice. Bob was a huge help to me in taking the necessary steps to do so.

Here are a few things I did for myself to promote more quality time and joy in my own life.

1. I became the priority. When you are in a highly stressful line of work and you are faced with some challenging demands on a daily basis, you make everyone else a priority except yourself. I rushed from one task to the next often fearful of what might or might not happen. I was really running on adrenaline (see chapter one). All that changed when I made myself my first priority.

2. I started to slow down. I learned the art of accepting that you can let certain things go. There is a difference in letting something go until another time, as opposed to being lazy and procrastinating. People who procrastinate don't start projects or do things, usually because they fear failure. Lazy people do not start a project because it requires work. I learned that some tasks can be left for another day. If, for example, the laundry doesn't get done today it can easily be done tomorrow.

3. I began to *say no*. I realized I did not have to be everything to everyone all of the time. If you are a people pleaser like me, this can be challenging. It took increased awareness to stop being a *yes* person. I didn't have to attend every function, party, event,

Constance Clancy-Fisher, EdD

and fund raiser. I didn't need to be a people pleaser anymore. This was empowering for me. Saying *no* used to be hard for me. As a pleaser, I thought I had to say *yes* to everyone in order for them to like me. As my confidence level increased, saying no became empowering for me. It felt uncomfortable initially, but then it reached a point where it really felt good to say no to things I truly wanted to say no to. I am very comfortable with it now. It has given me a freedom that I embrace. Remember that when setting a boundary with another, you may be tested, and that is fine. Once the other person realizes you really mean what you say, there will usually be a welcoming respect from them.

4. I learned how to unplug. I don't have to check my e-mails constantly anymore. I don't have to answer the phone every time it rings. I don't have to carry my cell phone everywhere I go. I don't have to have the television on constantly. These are distractions that I really don't want or need all the time in my daily life.

5. I started to honor my body. Women especially have a real challenge with this and I have been no exception. Leading fashion magazines have featured anorexic models on their covers, suggesting them as examples to be imitated. I learned that a healthy average weight is necessary to have a healthy body. I focused on things about my body that I like. The more I focused on what I liked, I found more about myself to like.

6. I started to eliminate activities such as excessive cleaning, shopping, exercising in hot weather because I thought I had to, and people who drained my energy. Some people are energy drainers, who take anything they can for their personal gain, including energy from other people. I learned to avoid them.

7. I started to practice *mindful living* everyday. Once I start thinking about the future, which takes me right out of the

present, my anxiety develops. Truly when I am in the moment, which is all I really have, mindfulness is experienced. I began a mindfulness practice by taking five minutes daily to sit, close my eyes, take a few deep breaths and just be. I increased the time and gradually worked up to thirty minutes, forty-five minutes, and even an hour.

8. I looked for opportunities to volunteer my services. Part of managing my time effectively includes taking the time to assist others. There are so many organizations looking for volunteers to assist in helping those in need. I would suggest volunteering for an organization for which you have a passion. Animal shelters, groups that help soldiers returning from war, or older veterans with mental and physical disabilities, homeless shelters, and soup kitchens always need people. I know people who volunteer on holidays when help is needed most. You will be glad you did, since it is another way to experience joy. You can volunteer for charity fundraisers in your community. Focusing on others in need, and helping to raise funding for those who are less fortunate, is a way to take the focus off your daily stressors and will help you realize how fortunate you are. Help others by volunteering. With so many in need, you can give of yourself and it just plain feels good. My husband and I had the good fortune of volunteering in the summer of 2011 at the Sopris Therapy Center Horses for Heros Program near Aspen, Colorado. We assisted the soldiers with overcoming their fear of riding horses and using their physical and mental disabilities to their advantage. Anyone who has worked with soldiers in this program knows how helpful it can be. Many soldiers suffer from *Post Traumatic Stress Disorder (PTSD)*. They need so much love and support. There are so many things in life that are so satisfying and rewarding, and volunteering is one of them.

Constance Clancy-Fisher, EdD

9. I stopped being fearful of what might or might not happen if I did or did not do something. I realized I was not managing my time effectively by incessant worry and fear. Fear can be paralyzing. When we are in fear, we don't feel love. If we don't feel love, we don't know how to give love to others. Fear is being outside the present moment. It means we are worried about the result of something that has already taken place, or anxious about the things that have yet to occur. Through meditation, I have allowed myself to contemplate and reflect on the biggest fears and challenges facing me. Upon reflection I concluded they were not that threatening.

My advice to you from the above includes:

+ When you set a boundary with another and he or she realizes you mean what you say, there will usually be a welcoming respect from them.

+ If you have a body image problem, start with just one attribute you like, certainly from the tips of your toes to the top of your head you can find one. Once you find one attribute, it will lead to finding others. Start doing things that make you feel good. Take a relaxing warm bath, a yoga class, or a dance lesson. Have a massage or a makeover. Give your body what it needs. Pay attention. Honor your body. Do your best to keep your body at an ideal weight to achieve optimal health.

+ If you tend to obsess about the future or stay focused on the past, you are NOT living mindfully in the present moment. Stay present and practice mindful living at your own pace.

Author Ram Dass says, "Deepen your practice of feeling fear, come close to it, invite it in for tea, and each time you do this, you will get a little closer to being able to look at it and say, "Ahhh, so." Thank you, Ram Dass.

"There is no such thing as a problem
Without a gift for you in its hands. You
Seek problems because you need their
Gifts."

RICHARD BACH

RELATIONSHIPS

As humans, we desire intimate, loving companionship. When we think of relationships, we typically think of romantic and intimate relations. In reality, we have relationships to ourselves, our parents, our siblings, our children, our friends and relatives, our pets, and our wife/husband/significant other. We also have relationships with the planet, home, colleagues, boss, religion, finances, food, among others.

Many people are challenged to find someone with whom to connect who can share the important moments of life. While most of us dream of manifesting that perfect person, we often end up discouraged and wondering why finding love and joy has to be so challenging.

For many, intimate relationships are our biggest challenge. We change relationships, and we end up having the same relationship issues, only with different people.

If people would begin to be truly aware that it is possible to give unconditionally of themselves and expect nothing in return, then a truly loving relationship can emerge. This awareness expands through loving more: the more loving one is, the more loving and joyful a relationship can be. We need to strive for mutual giving and receiving as opposed to focusing on getting something from the relationship.

When I work with couples in my counseling practice, it is because they disagree over issues they cannot resolve themselves. I invite each partner to tell why the couple has come for counseling. Then each is asked to describe what he or she has discovered about himself or herself as well as each other. This often leads to an understanding of each other's point of view and a willingness to compromise on a solution. Positive change can return joy to the relationship.

Consider this:

Bill and Sue met in college and fell madly in love. They decided to marry shortly after graduation. They each got jobs and within two years they had their first child.

They both came from divorced parents and vowed never to let this happen to them.

After a few years into the marriage, Bill began coming home later, saying he was working late at the office. Sue's suspicions grew as he became more distant. Their intimacy slacked off, and they began arguing more about little things. Bill was a good financial provider to the household, but for Sue, that was not enough. She was feeling neglected. Despite Sue's efforts to stay in shape and cook and clean on top of a full time job, she became exhausted and angry and lost all trust in Bill. One evening after Bill went to bed, she got on his computer and found e-mail exchanges between him and a female co-worker. Sue confronted Bill. He initially denied there was anything between him and his co-worker, but Sue did not believe him. Soon after, they went for counseling. Bill admitted to the counselor that the same scenario had happened with his own parents, and they eventually divorced due to infidelity in the marriage. Bill was filled with guilt and said that he loved Sue but was not "in love" with her anymore. He enjoyed the company of this other woman. While Bill knew consciously that this behavior was a repeat of his father's behavior, he still repeated the pattern that was set in his own family of origin. After a year of counseling and months of separation, Bill and Sue were able to save their marriage by working on the issues that contributed to the disaffection that had separated them. It took both of them to do the work together to make the marriage sustain. They both decided that they had too much invested, including a child whom they both loved dearly, to end it all. It took working through grief stages and forgiveness, which did not come easily or quickly. They also realized that to experience a joyful marriage, certain ways of living needed to be relinquished while other ways of living joyfully were developed and incorporated. What Sue realized through this episode was that she was a typically joyful individual and that joy came from within. She knew if the marriage didn't work that it would be sad and difficult to go on, but she would and the joy within her would emerge again. Bill was reaching outside himself for something external, which happened to be another person, to bring joy to him. He realized that this was a temporary fix and not true joy. He had to find that within himself. It was his own unrealistic expectations of himself that disappointed him and ultimately hurt their marriage. Sue's anger resolved when she stopped placing unrealistic expectations on Bill and learned to trust her own feelings again. They began to feel more love and acceptance with themselves and each other. The marriage began to thrive again, and love and joy returned to the relationship. If all scenarios turned out with happy endings like the one above, there would be fewer divorces. Sometimes when couples have tried everything, including counseling, and there still is no longer any desire to continue the relationship, then it is probably time for the couple to go their separate ways. When a relationship ends, I remind the spouses that there are gifts and learning that

Constance Clancy-Fisher, EdD

come out of any relationship, and they need to reflect and be aware of both.

I look back at all of my romantic relationships as gifts (although I did not see them as gifts at the time they ended), and I learned from each of them regardless of the hurt and suffering that I experienced when they ended. At this point in my life, I do not see them as anything to regret, rather I view them as an experience from which I gained much knowledge. Each relationship helped me grow in ways that made me better aware of what I wanted in relationship. I chose not to see them as failures because those relationships that gave me the impetus to realize the changes necessary to create the long lasting relationship for which I yearned.

Once you are in a relationship and can truly love and accept your partner, you can be genuine and authentic in ways you never could before. This is the kind of relationship that will evolve and grow. Healthy relationships have a mutual honor, respect and support. It's all about honoring each other. Partners don't have to agree on everything. You are not always going to want to do what your partner wants to do. Sometimes compromise is the solution, while at other times ceding a decision to the other makes sense when something is of great importance to the other. For example, you have plans to do something Friday night. "I thought we would go out to dinner then go to a movie." Your partner responds, "Oh, I was thinking we would have dinner in and watch a movie on TV." In a healthy relationship, partners know when to give in to the other, knowing that the other will reciprocate at the right time.

"What does relationship mean to you"? Take some time to think about this and write your response below.

WHAT RELATIONSHIP MEANS TO ME

_____

_____

_____

_____

_____

_____

_____

_____

_____

_____

_____

_____

_____

_____

_____

I asked friends, family, colleagues, and clients what relationship means to them. Here are some responses.

*Note: The names have been changed.

Adrianna: "It is listening to someone with compassion and letting them know you are present with them."

Jay: "Relationship to me means being able to tell your partner anything, knowing you will be accepted and not be judged."

Carol: "Relationship is about giving and receiving."

Mark: "I think relationship is nurturing those you care for and accepting them for however human they are."

Laurie: "Relationship means to me the giving of one's self, from the heart, that will allow both persons to freely open up and love."

Judy: "Relationship means opening up and giving everything unselfishly to my children."

Ian: "Relationship to me is at its greatest when we stop trying to change the other person."

Affirmations to Consider in Relationships
+ I allow myself to have a loving relationship that supports me in my freedom and aliveness.
+ I allow myself to let go of expectations.
+ I allow myself to have the perfect relationship for me.
+ I allow my relationships to be loving and supportive.
+ I allow my relationships to be full of honor and respect.
+ I allow myself to give and receive love.

CHAPTER FIVE

*How The Stress Of Aging Changes
To The Gift Of Years*

"**Whether we live to a vigorous old age lies not
So much in our stars or in our genes as in
Ourselves.**"

GEORGE VAILLANT

FROM BIRTH UNTIL DEATH, WE experience a series of developmental stages throughout our life. We develop characteristics based on the challenges faced and support we received growing up. Below are developmental stages of life humans go through. They were posited by the late social scientist Erik Erikson. He suggested that the course of development is determined by the interaction of the body (genetic biological programming), mind (psychological), and cultural (ethos) influences. As you read through these stages, try to determine where you now in your own development. While this chapter focuses on the aging process and how your remaining years can be full of productivity and gifts, reviewing Erikson's stages of development can provide an understanding of how your early life led you to where you are in your life now. Each stage carries significance.

1. Birth to 18 Months: Trust vs. Mistrust. If we pass successfully through this stage of life, we learn to trust that life is basically okay and have basic confidence in the future.
2. Early Childhood: 18 Months to 3 Years. Autonomy vs. Shame. We have the opportunity to develop self-esteem and autonomy as we gain more control over our bodies and acquire new skills, learning right from wrong.
3. Play Age: 3 to 5 Years: Initiative vs. Guilt. During this stage we experience a desire to copy the adults around us and take initiative in creating play situations. We begin to question why. If we become frustrated over natural desires and goals, we may experience guilt.
4. School Age: 6 to 12 Years: Industry vs. Inferiority. During this stage, often called Latency, we are capable of learning, creating and accomplishing numerous new skills and knowledge, thus developing a sense of industry. This is also a very social stage of development, and if we experience unresolved feelings of inadequacy and inferiority among our peers, we can have problems in terms of competence and self-esteem.
5. Adolescence: 12 to 18 Years. Identity vs. Role Confusion. According to Erikson, development mostly depends upon what is done to us. From this stage on, development depends primarily on what we do. Life becomes more complex as we attempt to find our own identity, struggle with social interactions, and grapple with moral issues. If we are unsuccessful in navigating this stage, we will experience role confusion and upheaval.

6. Young Adulthood: 18 to 35 Years. Intimacy and Solidarity vs. Isolation. As adults, we try to find mutually satisfying relationships, primarily through marriage and friends. We generally also begin to start a family. If this stage is successful, we can experience intimacy on a deep level. If unsuccessful, isolation and distance from others may occur.

7. Middle Adulthood: 35 to 55 or 65 Years. Generativity vs. Self-absorption or Stagnation. Now work is most crucial. We tend to be occupied with creative and meaningful work and with issues surrounding our family. Middle adulthood is when we can expect to "be in charge." Strength comes through care of others and production of something that contributes to the betterment of society according to Erikson. As our children leave home, or our relationships or goals change, we may be faced with major life changes. Midlife crisis and struggle with finding new meaning and purpose in life. If we don't get through this stage successfully, we can become self-absorbed and stagnate.

8. Late Adulthood: 55 or 65 to Death. Integrity vs. Despair. As older adults, we often look back on our lives with happiness and are content, feeling as though we have made a contribution to life, a feeling Erikson calls integrity. On the other hand, some adults may reach this stage and despair at their experiences and perceived failures. They may fear death as they struggle to find a purpose to their lives. We can choose to live joyfully well into our 80's and 90's without despair. The choice is ours.

When I was working on my doctoral degree (1987 to 1990), a colleague of mine made the comment, "How can you be so young and so wise?" I seemed young to her, and I suppose I was. I was in my early 30's and the rest of the class was at least 40 and older. Now that seems so long ago and I am so much older! Yet, I was

Constance Clancy-Fisher, EdD

hiking this morning and while I was on a little more challenging trail, I thought to myself, "I feel every bit as good now as I did when I was 20." So I believe what it really boils down to is our attitude when it comes to the aging process. As my friend Natalie says, "We're not like our mothers or grandmothers." Now, 60 is the new 40, and 50 is the new 30 and so on. We don't see many women in their 60's sitting in rockers with short curly blue-gray hair like the women we remember from our childhoods. My friends in their 60's are attractive, active, slim, and well, sexy. We can thank the baby boomers for this. What incredible things they have done for anti-aging.

In July of 2012, my husband Bob and I were walking in Aspen, Colorado. He pointed and said, "There goes a young Connie." Sure enough, I saw a younger version of myself. She was about 30 years my junior, pony tail, appeared fit and was walking two dogs, right down to the same breed and colors of mine. It took me aback for a moment, as I couldn't believe that I am now in my mid-fifties! It doesn't seem possible I thought. It seems like yesterday that I was that young girl in my 20's. I remember so much of that part of my life so clearly. Instead of thinking that I was old, I embraced the moment, and wished that younger version of me to have as many wonderful experiences as I have had. I also thought, *Gee, I feel great and I am still enjoying as much now if not more than I did then.* It would be wonderful if we could all feel that way as we age. We need to remember that attitude is an important factor that helps determine who we become as we age. Do we welcome aging or do we fear it? We will need to look at our fears as well as our hopes, wishes and dreams.

"It's not the crows feet under your eyes that make you old,
Or the gray in your hair I'm told. But when your mind
Makes a contract that your body cannot fulfill, you're
Over the hill brother, you're over the hill."

RAM DASS'S FATHER

THE NATURE OF AGING

In our culture there is no clear rite of passage through middle age into old age. Some think it is when you develop gray hair or wrinkles, or need to use a cane. True, in our older years we are faced with physical, psychological, economic and spiritual changes. Normal physical aging includes:

+ Hormonal changes
+ Muscle mass decline
+ Inflammatory changes
+ A decrease in maximum heart rate in response to exercise

Age-related infirmities include arthritis, insomnia, poor circulation, high cholesterol, joint discomfort, muscle atrophy, vision and hearing loss, and more, depending on the individual. Many new discoveries can help minimize these changes, allowing us to remain active and physically healthy into our senior years. Aging brings changes that can challenge us emotionally. Forgetfulness and frailty can lead to loss of self-confidence and anxiety. Loss of a loved one can trigger depression and despair. As your social support system changes, you try to hold onto things as they are, to maintain some security. It's hard to accept that things in our lives change. If you can realize that it's your own identification with these thoughts and feelings that are the cause of your suffering, you can be more accepting of life's changes. Especially now with uncertain economic times, many boomers are downsizing. They realize they don't need all the stuff they once thought they did. Two-household

Constance Clancy-Fisher, EdD

couples are downsizing to much more now than a decade ago. They also are living on less money, having lost pensions, exhausted their retirement savings, or realized very little from investments. Be mindful that it's not so much the changes but our attitude toward them that can make or break this special time in our lives.

There are many activities for seniors to enjoy. For example, Elder Hostel, also known as Road Scholar, is a not-for-profit organization that offers senior citizens educational and travel opportunities. For those seniors who are not interested in or are unable to travel, retirement communities have much to offer that range from active physical participation to lectures and discussion groups.

"Death is Life's Change Agent."

Steve Jobs

My great uncle lived to be 90. I used to tell him I thought it would be so cool if he lived to be 100. Then he could be on the Today Show with Willard Scott. His reply was, "I don't want to live that long. All my friends are gone, and I have lived a full life."

As we age we face the loss of our friends. When we lose most of our friends, loneliness can set in. We all face loss of family members with whom we are especially close. In 1990, my uncle was almost 91 years old and I had almost finished my doctoral program.

He became ill and very weak, unable to take care of himself anymore. He was admitted to a residential care facility. He had always said that he would not last long in a facility and he would be ready to leave the earth. I visited him there, and he asked me if I was finished with my doctorate. I replied that I was finishing and I would have my official degree within the month. He lived to hear the news that pleased him so much. He had been supportive of my higher education. Then ready to depart, he died the next week. He had no fear of dying and we had many discussions about what we thought passing on was like. He was a man who lived with integrity (Erikson's last developmental stage of life), not despair. I don't think there is any greater gift. Perhaps we can think of aging as a journey of gaining knowledge leading to wisdom. If our physical body remains healthy, that is a beautiful gift. If our physical health diminishes, we accept that, and can still continue our quest of knowledge. Many find aging leads to examination of the spiritual aspect of ourselves. Elders make up a large portion of religious congregations. Other cultures revere their elders because of their wisdom; we can, too.

**"When you lose your fear of
Death, you gain a love for life."**

RAM DASS

Author *Ram Dass*, in his book *Still Here*, writes about embracing aging, changing and dying. He is known as a man who blazed a spiritual path for his generation and continues to bring wisdom, humor and after his stroke a new perspective that takes us through the aging journey and beyond. Ram Dass explains that the key spiritual work, that aging well requires, is the way in which we relate to death. The spiritual journey awakens you to a new awareness of life. Once we gain recognition that we are one aspect of the whole, we will be able to look directly at death as a part of life.

The late Sir David R. Hawkins, M.D., Ph.D., is a nationally renowned psychiatrist, researcher, lecturer and author. Dr. Hawkins' books and lectures (available from Veritas Pub.com), are invaluable for all who are on the path to enlightenment.

Constance Clancy-Fisher, EdD

Dr. Hawkins' research on the Nature of Consciousness led to the development of the Map of Consciousness (a qualitative and quantitative analysis and calibration of the levels of consciousness). The map gives us a numerical calibration of the vibrational values of the different emotions and the level of consciousness we are at when experiencing that emotion, e.g., when we have the emotion of "Hate," our level of consciousness is "Fear," and our view of life is "Antagonistic." If our emotion is "Forgiveness", our level of consciousness is "Acceptance," and our life view is "Harmonious." The Map of Consciousness is also available from the website previously mentioned. It is my feeling that this information will lead to a greater understanding of the material presented in this book.

COMING ALIVE

Being older can be a time to come alive in ways we have never done before.

So many think that when their body deteriorates, they are "falling apart" and it's all over. Not so. There is a whole new creative part of the self that can emerge if the mind allows and accepts what is. Take Larry for example. He is 89 and he still drives a car, he lives alone in his own home, eats well, exercises at the fitness center three times a week, attends classes and discussion groups.

Actress Jane Fonda in her book *Prime Time* writes about the eleven ingredients that help us to age successfully. Experts, friends, and things that she has learned from her own life experience contributed to the following:

1. Not abusing alcohol
2. Not smoking
3. Getting enough sleep
4. Eating a healthy diet
5. Maintaining a healthy, active brain through constantly learning new things

6. Keeping a positive mental attitude
7. Being physically active
8. Reviewing and reflecting on your own life to be aware of changes you may want to make
9. Loving and staying connected with others
10. Giving of oneself
11. Caring about the bigger picture

"Every person, all the events in your life
Are there because you've drawn them there.
What you choose to do with them is up to you."

RICHARD BACH

THE BLESSINGS OF AGING

Often when we embrace the changes of aging, we begin to see the true meaning and purpose of life. So what lies ahead is something we can choose. We can decide how to grow in new ways. We can spend some time in reflection and contemplation. We don't realize what a blessing that is until we reach out to others and do something. Aging is meant for us to engage with others, start new projects, and be creative in how we allow our lives to become more meaningful. As my wise husband Bob says, "Present time consciousness takes us into the center of ourselves."

As a therapist, I have witnessed too many older folks think that they are no longer any value to society. They consider themselves useless because they believe they are no longer contributing to society as they once did when they were working. I suggest that they can become involved in helping others in many capacities.

Stereotypes of Aging in our Western Culture

We Westerners for the most part have difficulty with the aging process. In our culture, we are not taught about aging; therefore, we are unprepared to embrace aging as well as we could. Just look at our television commercials. They try to sell us age-defying wrinkle creams, lotions and serums, as well as weight-loss pills and gadgets to tone the tummy and give us 6-pack abs. The fashion and celebrity magazines are so youth-oriented they make it seem as if aging never happens. It is something we have to hide.

In Japan, silver hair and wrinkles are not looked down upon, and wisdom and service are valued. Will we Westerners ever get to that place?

Scientists have recently discovered that the adult brain can adapt itself to compensate for damage, such as may occur from a stroke, for instance, by producing new neural networks, a phenomenon known as "plasticity." What is even more exciting, researchers have found that the brain, known to suffer from the regular death of cells through aging, also experiences the growth of new cells. Older people can be as mentally competent as their younger counterparts and, often, have greater depth and wisdom from accumulated experience. They can offer compassion, kindness, and guidance to those younger in a society that values their contributions. Perhaps you are at a crossroads, facing retirement or advancing age. At these crossroads we can either be consumed with fear or excited about entering a new phase of life filled with adventure and new beginnings. Carl Jung warned of being too occupied with the self later in life. Older age and retirement offer us the chance to be of service to others, which in turn, provides the rewards that service to others brings. Our country needs its people, vibrant and contributing at every stage of life.

"Don't be dismayed at goodbyes. A farewell is necessary
Before you can meet again. And meeting again,
After moments or lifetimes, is certain for those who are
Friends."

RICHARD BACH

CONCLUSION

"Acknowledge yourself for being centered when
There is incredible chaos around you. Acknowledge
Yourself for being courageous and doing so much
More than you thought you could."

LOUISE HAY

THE ULTIMATE GOAL OF CHANGE

The ultimate goal of change is to recognize that change within the world comes from change within the individual. Our planet is facing many challenges: diminishment of resources, pollution, over population, just to name a few. We all individually and collectively need to realize that in some way we contribute to the planet's growing problems. If we do not find long-term solutions, quality of human life will certainly diminish. If we all work together, we will find and implement these long-term solutions so our children and grandchildren and all future generations can live in harmony with their environment. Each one of us can begin today to educate ourselves on all the ways we can help, such as recycling, using products that do not pollute the environment, growing food, using fuel-efficient vehicles, and buying products that last. We can be the answer instead of the problem. As we become proactive we will live with less stress and more joy. When we accept and embrace the challenge of change without resistance, helping our neighbor will be the norm. We will use the challenge of change to benefit all humanity. It's when we can begin to become aware of the change we can make from within that we will live with less stress and more joy. It is when we embrace and accept the challenge of change freely, without resistance, that our life will come alive. We will feel more whole and complete, perhaps experiencing an energy shift that may take our lives to a whole new level. When we can live in the world without demanding it fill our every need, we will have found a new way of living in it. When we realize it is not the responsibility of others to make us happy, we will have reached the level of awareness that true happiness comes from within. When we feel unconditional love and compassion for all creation, we walk on the path to enlightenment.

Organizations For Information

ON STRESS MANAGEMENT, CHANGE, HEALING AND TRANSFORMATION

American Association of Oriental Medicine
P.O. 162340
Sacramento, CA 95816
916-443-4770
www.aaom.org

American Association of Integrative Medicine
2750 East Sunshine Street
Springfield, MO
877-718-3053
www.aaimedicine.com

American Holistic Medical Association
6728 Old McLean Village Drive
McLean, VA 22101
703-556-9728
www.holisticmedicine.org

Barbara Brennan School of Healing
500 NE Spanish River Boulevard #208
Boca Raton, FL 33431
www.barbarabrennan.com

Benson-Henry Institute for Mind Body Medicine
151 Merrimac Street
Boston, MA 02114
617-643-6090
www.massgeneral.org/bhi/

Center for Mindfulness in Medicine
University of Massachusetts Medical School
55 Lake Avenue North
Worcester, MA 06155
508-856-2656
www.umassmed.edu

Colorado Center for Healing Touch
Healing Touch International
12477 West Cedar Drive
Lakewood, CO 80228
303-989-7982
www.healingtouchprogram.com

Health Journeys
891 Moe Drive Suite C
Akron, OH 44310
330-633-3831
www.healthjourneys.com

Inspiration Unlimited and Paramount Wellness Institute
P.O. Box 18831
Boulder, CO 80308
303-678-9962
www.brianlukeseaward.net

Institute of Noetic Sciences
101 San Antonio Road
Petaluma, CA 94952
707-775-3500
www.instituteofnoeticsciences.com

Island Chiropractic Center
2400 Palm Ridge Road C-3
Sanibel Island, FL 33957
239-472-6032
robertfisherdc@gmail.com

Kirpalu Center for Yoga and Health
57 Interlaken Road
Stockbridge, MA 01240
413-448-3400
www.kirpalu.org

National Center for Complementary and Alternative Medicine
P.O. Box 7923
Gaithersberg, MD 20898
888-644-6226
http://nccam.nih.gov

National Guild of Hypnotists, Inc.
P.O. Box 308
Merrimack, NH 03054
603-429-9438
www.ngh.net

National Institutes of Health
9000 Rockville Pike
Bethesda, MD 20892
888-644-6226
www.nih.gov

National Wellness Institute, Inc.
P.O. Box 827
Stevens Point, WI 54481
715-342-2969
www.nationalwellness.org

Omega Institute for Holistic Studies
150 Lake Drive
Rhinebeck, NY 12572
877-944-2002
www.omega.org

The Energy Medicine Institute
777 East Main Street
Ashland, OR 97520
541-482-1800
www.energymed.org

The Humor Potential, Inc.
50 Court Street
Plymouth, MA 02360
508-746-3998
www.stressed.com

Veritas Publishing (Dr. David Hawkins' Books, CD's etc.)
P.O. Box 3516
W. Sedona, AZ 86340
928-282-8722

Bibliography

American Association of Integrative Medicine, JAAIM-Online: "Herbs and Their Uses" (July 2012). http: //www.aaimedicine. com.

American Dietetic Association (ADA), Food and Nutrition (September Conference, 2011).

American Psychological Association, Stress and Burnout Statistics: Physical and Psychological Symptoms of Anxiety and Stress (Study, 2007).

American University School of Communication, Mood of the Country: 'Anxiety Ridden' by Lynne Peri (October, 2011).

Benson, Herbert. M.D., and Miriam Z. Klipper, *The Relaxation Response* (New York: Berkley, 1976).

Bodin, Stephen, *Meditation for Dummies* (California: IDG Books, 1999).

Chodron, Pema, *Comfortable with Uncertainty* (Massachusetts: Shambala Publications, 2003).

Clancy, Constance, *Surviving Stress with a Healing Heart* (Florida: First Publish, 2002).

Cousins, Norman, *Head First: The Biology of Hope* (New York: Harper & Row, 1989).

Dass, Ram, *Still Here: Embracing Aging, Changing and Dying* (New York: Riverhead Books, 2000).

DeAngelis, Barbara, *How Did I Get Here?* (Virginia: Holtzbrinck Publishers, LLC, 2005).

Dyer, Wayne, *Manifest Your Destiny* (New York: Harper Collins, 1997).

Ellis, Albert, Windy Dryden, *The Practice of Rational Emotive Behavior Therapy* (New York: Springer Publishers, July, 2007)

Fonda, Jane, *Prime Time* (New York: Random House, 2011).

Hay, Louise, *The Power is Within You* (California: Hay House, 1991).

His Holiness the Dalai Lama, *How to Expand Love* (New York: Atria Books, 2005).

Internet Article, United States Satisfaction with Government, Morality, Economy Down since 2008. Gallup Poll, 2011.

Kabat-Zinn, Jon, *Wherever You Go, There You Are* (New York: Hyperion, 1994).

Katie, Byron, *A Thousand Names for Joy* (New York: Harmony Books, 2007).

Klemens, Jonathan, *Using Herbs Wisely: A Basic Primer* (Pennsylvania: Health &

Fitness, May, 2000).

Kubler-Ross, Elisabeth, *On Death and Dying*, Elisabeth Kubler-Ross, 1969.

LaRoche, Loretta, *Relax: You May Only Have a Few Minutes Left* (New York: Villard, 1998).

Mindell, Earl, *Herb Bible* (New York: Simon & Schuster/Fireside, 1992).

Myss, Carolyn, *Sacred Contracts: Awakening Your Divine Potential* (New York: Crown Publishing Group, 2003).

Naparstek, Belleruth, *Staying Well With Guided Imagery* (New York: Werner Books, 1995).

Northrup, Christiane, *Women's Bodies, Women's Wisdom* (New York: Random House, 2010).

Peck, M. Scott, *The Road Less Traveled*, 25th Anniversary Edition (New York: Simon & Schuster, 2002).

Rechtschaffen, Stephen and Marc Cohen, *Vitality and Wellness*, Omega Institute (New York: Dell Publishing, 1999).

Richardson, Cheryl, *Take Time For Your Life* (New York: Broadway Books, 1999).

Roth, Geneen, *Women, Food and God*, (New York: Scribner Publishers, 2011).

Seaward, Brian Luke, *Managing Stress: Principles and Strategies for Health and Well-Being* (Massachusetts:Jones & Bartlett, 2009).

Seaward, Brian Luke, *Stand Like Mountain, Flow Like Water* (Florida: Health Communications Publishing, 1997).

Seaward, Brian Luke, *Stressed is Desserts Spelled Backward* (California: Conari Press; 1st Edition, July, 1999).

The New York Times Upfront, Was It Necessary to Drop the Bomb on Japan?

Gar Alperovitz, Professor of Political Essay, University of Maryland, 2012.

Thich Nhat Hahn, *Peace is Every Step*, (New York: Bantam Books, 1991).

Tolle, Eckhart, *A New Earth*, (Florida: Namaste Publishing, 2005).

Warren, Neil Clark, *Make Anger Your Ally*, (Colorado: Living Books, 1993).

About The Author

CONSTANCE CLANCY-FISHER, ED.D., IS A licensed mental health counselor (LMHC) and hypnotherapist who has been in private practice for over twenty years. Connie has presented and continues to present stress reduction seminars, mindfulness meditation, healing workshops and retreats throughout the country. She is a local newspaper columnist for the Sanibel Island Sun and writes a weekly question and answer column.

Connie maintains a private counseling practice and divides her time between Sanibel Island and Snowmass, Colorado. She lives with her husband, Robert Fisher, D.C., her two yellow Labrador Retrievers, Ana and Ari, and Snookie the cat.

For additional information on consultations, seminars, retreats and counseling services, please contact Connie at 970-376-4163. www. drconstance.com, e-mail: connie@drconstance.com

22390617R00094

Made in the USA
Lexington, KY
27 April 2013